TEACHING and LEARNING
With DIGITAL
PHOTOGRAPHY

*This book is dedicated to my grandchildren
(Courtney, Molly, and Christian), who were
responsible for inspiring me to develop my skills
with digital technology to document their growth
and to capture special moments. It's especially dedicated
to Courtney, who already is a better photographer
than I am. I also dedicate this book to those parents
and professionals who use this book and will be
inspired to find other applications of digital
photography in their lives and work.*

TEACHING and LEARNING With DIGITAL PHOTOGRAPHY

Tips and Tools for Early Childhood Classrooms

LINDA GOOD

CORWIN PRESS
A SAGE Company
Thousand Oaks, CA 91320

For information:

Corwin Press
A SAGE Company
2455 Teller Road
Thousand Oaks, California 91320
www.corwinpress.com

SAGE India Pvt. Ltd.
B 1/I 1 Mohan Cooperative
    Industrial Area
Mathura Road, New Delhi 110 044
India

SAGE Ltd.
1 Oliver's Yard
55 City Road
London EC1Y 1SP
United Kingdom

SAGE Publications
    Asia-Pacific Pte. Ltd.
33 Pekin Street #02-01
Far East Square
Singapore 048763

Printed in the United States of America.

Library of Congress Cataloging-in-Publication Data

Good, Linda.
Teaching and learning with digital photography: tips and tools for early childhood classrooms/Linda Good.
    p. cm.
Includes bibliographical references and index.
ISBN 978-1-4129-6075-5 (cloth)
ISBN 978-1-4129-6076-2 (pbk.)
    1. Early childhood education—United States. 2. Photography—Digital techniques. 3. Technology and children—United States. I. Title.

LB1139.25.G66 2009
372.133'52—dc22   2008019172

This book is printed on acid-free paper.

08   09   10   11   12   10   9   8   7   6   5   4   3   2   1

Acquisitions Editor:	Jessica Allan
Editorial Assistant:	Joanna Coelho
Production Editor:	Eric Garner
Copy Editor:	Paula L. Fleming
Typesetter:	C&M Digitals (P) Ltd.
Proofreader:	Kevin Gleason
Indexer:	Sheila Bodell
Cover Designer:	Monique Hahn

Contents

Foreword

WHO SHOULD READ AND USE THIS BOOK?

This book is primarily designed to assist early childhood educators who teach preschoolers, kindergartners, or primary-grade children to integrate digital images into teaching. Although the text is not directed at parents, parents may find some of the applications pertinent to their role as their child's first teacher. Another population that would benefit from the book and CD are preservice teachers or college students who are in the process of becoming professional educators. Additionally, teacher educators might use this as a text for college coursework, and trainers might use it as a resource.

THIS BOOK IS . . .

This book is a compendium of concrete examples for integrating digital technology, specifically digital images such as photographs and clip art, into curriculum and assessment materials, as well as into tools for communicating with parents. The ideas presented are applicable to all children. That is, young children with special needs, except those with vision deficits, benefit from the use of photos in the same way that any young child benefits. In some instances, using photos assists some special populations; these will be noted in the text. English-language learners also benefit from seeing photos, because they can provide a context for understanding English as a foreign language. Children who are pictured in the examples are both typically and atypically developing children and both English-language speakers and English-language learners.

After establishing a theoretical foundation for using this type of technology in early childhood environments, the reader is given an overview of hardware, software, and consumables to get started in using digital images. The primary software application that is demonstrated throughout the book is PowerPoint. Typically part of the Microsoft Office Suite software package, PowerPoint is one of the most available software programs for both Macintosh and PC users. However, other software applications are mentioned.

A variety of applications is presented, from documenting growth to integrating digital photos into curriculum areas. The reader will be guided to use the PowerPoint application as a means of developing materials. Suggestions for using digital photos to enhance development in all the developmental domains (social/emotional development, language development, cognitive development, and motor development) and typical primary subject areas are offered. Additionally, guidelines for using digital images to communicate with parents, as well as for documenting children's growth and development in a pictorial portfolio, are presented. The reader will learn how photos can assist with classroom management, promote language and literacy, and be used to develop curriculum materials. Children can use cameras, too, as a parent/child activity entitled "Take Home Snappy!" Digital photos can be utilized to communicate with staff about how to use materials with children. Photo images can be used for a variety of fundraisers. Digital technology can assist teachers and parents in the important work they do to help all children grow, develop, and gain skills.

This book presents many applications for digital photography, but there are many more uses for readers to discover on their own. When one becomes adept at using digital images, a new vista of possibilities presents itself. It is hoped that using digital images will increase your imagination as you are inspired to use your own creativity and expand the boundaries of what is presented here.

THIS BOOK IS NOT . . .

This book is not a how-to manual for selecting or using digital cameras or other equipment, nor is it book to teach computer literacy skills. Although some technological hardware and software are discussed briefly, it is up to the readers to investigate these further on their own. It is expected that users have some basic computer literacy skills.

THE CD IS . . .

The CD is a supplement to the book. It contains many user-friendly templates so that busy child care providers, teachers, and parents can readily and quickly implement some of the ideas presented in the book. The PowerPoint platform is used for the templates. The CD also contains Microsoft Word document versions of forms that are presented in the book.

THE CD IS NOT . . .

The CD is not a complete collection of everything that the early childhood educator, primary-grade teacher, college student or instructor, professional trainer, or parent might do with digital images. However, it is hoped that the examples presented on the CD will be modified or expanded by the users as they gain confidence and competence in utilizing them. Because of copyright issues, clip art is not demonstrated on the CD; only the author's original photos are used.

Acknowledgments

A work such as this cannot be attributed to the authors alone. It takes collaboration and consultation to bring such a work to fruition. Although I had played with my camera and developed many applications, I did not realize that I might have something unique to share with others until I met Conny Li. Conny Li, from the Hong Kong Bureau of Education and Manpower, invited me to come to Hong Kong and conduct workshops with some of the preschool teachers there. Conny was the person who suggested that I develop templates; her idea not only sparked the development of the templates but also became the catalyst for writing this book.

As I was developing the templates and the book, I was inspired by the preschool children and teachers with whom I work in the Mankato, Minnesota, area as well as the students in the Early Childhood Education Program at Minnesota State University—Mankato. They were my allies as I tried out new ideas. The children from Montessori Learning Center, Covenant Christian Child Care Center, and District 77 Special Education classrooms were willing subjects who joyously greeted me each time I appeared with my camera. I appreciate that their parents gave me permission to photograph them. I also express my gratitude to Dianne Armbrust, who has become an advocate for my work and whose enthusiasm is spreading to others as she uses the CD to produce digital books in a literacy program that she manages.

My colleague, Dr. Ron Browne, collaborated with me early on as I explored applications; he explained camera and computer features and taught me useful skills. Another colleague, Dr. John Solis, freely offered advice and assistance with the technical features of this book and agreed to write the technical portions. Graduate student Tessa Donato enthusiastically assisted with translating some of the text on the templates into Spanish; I am so appreciative of her contribution so that we might extend the applications to another population.

I would be remiss not to mention all the people and reviewers at Corwin Press who helped to bring this book and CD to reality. They excitedly greeted my work and offered constructive suggestions to improve my product.

The encouragement of family and friends was also important, because writing a book is a long process that consumes time and energy. The people nearest and dearest to me gave me time and space to work. They also allowed me to use family photos to illustrate some of my examples.

Additionally, Corwin Press would like to acknowledge the following peer reviewers for their editorial insight and guidance:

Deborah Alexander-Davis
Former Elementary Teacher and Principal,
    Roane County Schools, TN
2004 Tennessee Principal of the Year
Adjunct Professor, Tennessee Technological
    University, Cookeville, TN

Carrie Carpenter
Coordinator
Deschutes Edge Charter School
Redmond, OR

Teresa Cunningham
Principal
Laurel Elementary School
Laurel Bloomery, TN

Jane Ching Fung
Educator
Alexander Science Center School
Los Angeles, CA

Sue DeLay
Learning Support Teacher
Cedar Hills Elementary School
Oak Creek, WI

Carol Forrest
Kindergarten to First-Grade Teacher
Nyssa Elementary School
Nyssa, OR

Jenni Harding-DeKam
Assistant Professor
University of Northern Colorado
Greeley, CO

Sharon Judge
Associate Dean
Old Dominion University
Norfolk, VA

Alexis Ludewig
2002 Wisconsin Teacher of the Year
Third-Grade Teacher
Land O'Lakes School
Land O'Lakes, WI

About the Author

 **Linda Good** received her PhD from the University of Minnesota in 1990. She is currently a professor of Early Childhood Education at Minnesota State University—Mankato, where she serves as the coordinator of the Early Childhood Education Program. Previous to her present position, she was an associate professor at South Dakota State University and an assistant professor at the University of South Dakota. Recently, she served as an exchange professor at the Catholic University of Daegu in South Korea.

Prior to working full-time in higher education, she served many roles in the early childhood profession. She was a coordinator of Early Childhood Family Education, a long-term substitute home-based teacher for Head Start, and a teacher of young children with special needs.

Linda is very involved in local, state, and regional early childhood organizations and has served as president of the South Dakota Association for the Education of Young Children, been an active board member of both the South Dakota and Minnesota Associations for the Education of Young Children, and served as the Midwest Council representative from both South Dakota and Minnesota with the Midwest Association for the Education of Young Children. She is affiliated with the National Association for the Education of Young Children, Association of Childhood Education International, and the National Association of Early Childhood Teacher Educators. She presents locally, regionally, nationally, and internationally. She has authored several articles and one other book.

She is a widow, a mother, and a grandmother. She lives on a lake in Minnesota and enjoys her grandchildren, travel, reading, and swimming.

Part I

The Rationale for Integrating Digital Photography Into Early Childhood Education Practices

Rhyme and Reasons

1

Snap my photo; take a picture of me
Take my photo, and let me see
I like to look on the LCD
So, teacher, please snap a picture of me.

Look at my picture in a book
It makes me want to look and look
On the wall is another photo of me
It makes me feel like part of this community

The use of the digital camera as a teaching tool in early childhood education is gaining momentum. Chip Donohue (2003), the director of Early Childhood Professional Development Programs at the University of Wisconsin—Milwaukee, states: "Trends to watch in technology tools for teaching young children can easily be summed up—digital technologies and the Internet" (p. 20). Murphy, DePasquale, and McNamara (2003) say that "digital imagery is one of the most exciting technological applications for early childhood classrooms" (p. 13). Theoretical frameworks that contribute to the foundations of developmentally appropriate practice can be used as a rationale for the use of technological tools in early childhood education. Professional organizations support the use of technological tools by teachers and young children. The ease and applicability of digital imagery in early childhood education make it a desirable tool. All of these contribute to the "whys" of using digital images in early childhood education.

DEVELOPMENTAL AND INSTRUCTIONAL THEORIES

Theoretical frameworks supply the rationale for many practices in early childhood education. Because no one theory can adequately explain development, it is recognized that many theorists have contributed to understanding how children learn. So, too, one can look to multiple theoretical frameworks to give a rationale for using photographic images in early childhood education. Although many of the theoretical foundations that drive developmentally appropriate practices in early childhood education were formulated before technology offered easy access to creating and using images, the theories nonetheless support the use of images in early childhood education.

Some developmental theorists whose work supports the use of images in the early learning environment include Maslow, Goleman, Erikson, Vygotsky, and Piaget. The work of instructional theorists like Montessori, Bruner, Gardner, Gagné, and Keller also offers rationale for using digital images. The relationships of these theorists' concepts and the use of digital photography are summarized in Table 1.1.

Maslow's Hierarchy of Needs

Abraham Maslow (1968) postulated that humans have basic needs that must be met for learning to occur. Once a child's physiological and safety needs are met, the need for love and belonging emerges on the next tier of Maslow's hierarchy of needs. This need for "belongingness" is then a prerequisite for the next tier: esteem. Esteem is earned from success and status. For children to achieve success, they must first feel that they fit into the community of learners.

Belongingness has been translated into the construct of classrooms as communities of learners in which all members have a place and a space. When children can see their spaces (cubbies or lockers) defined with photos of themselves as well as a labeling with their names, children can immediately sense that they belong there. When children can see a photo of themselves as members of a class depicted on a bulletin board, as shown in Figure 1.1, they feel included in that group. When children can look around the room and see that they are some of the characters featured in a book or in a puzzle, the children know that they belong. The children feel welcomed into the world of the classroom, and they develop a sense of belonging in this environment.

Another interpretation of *belongingness* is that of inclusion. Many teachers strive to make all children feel welcome in their classrooms. Typically one strategy to provide a welcoming atmosphere is to put up

Table 1.1   Theories Reinforced With Digital Photography

Developmental Theorists	Theory	Concepts Associated With This Theory	How Digital Photos Reinforce the Theoretical Constructs
Abraham Maslow	Hierarchy of Needs	Need for "belongingness"; inclusion	Photos of membership
Daniel Goleman	Emotional Intelligence	Self-awareness of feelings	Photographs of emotions
Erik Erikson	Psychosocial Development	Stage 3: initiative versus guilt	Photos to picture choices and to guide an activity
Lev Vygotsky	Socio-Cultural Cognitive Development	Assisted learning in zone of proximal development	Photos used in process charts
Jean Piaget	Constructivist Cognitive Development	Egocentrism as characteristic of preoperational child	Photos of children to engage them in materials
Instructional Theorists			
Maria Montessori	Montessori Method	Practical life: autonomous learning	Process charts using photos
Jerome Bruner	Cognitive Development	Enactive, iconic, and symbolic mentalities; scaffolding learning	Photographic images as icons
Howard Gardner	Multiple Intelligences	Intrapersonal intelligence	Photos of children so they can see themselves and reflect on what is pictured
Gagné	Levels and Conditions of Learning	Events of instruction	Photos as aids to instruction and generalization
Keller	Motivational Model	Attention, relevance, confidence, and satisfaction	Personal photos as visual aids and motivators for learning

Figure 1.1   Bulletin Board of Members of the Brown Class

posters of children of various genders, sizes, racial and ethnic groups, and abilities. In today's inclusive classrooms populated by children of varying abilities and cultural and racial differences, it is not difficult to picture diversity by posting photos of the children actually present in the early childhood environment.

Goleman's Emotional Quotient Theory

More recent advocacy for this sense of belongingness could be related to Goleman's (1995) emotional quotient theory. Goleman states that we have both a thinking brain and a feeling brain, based on the research on brain development and brain functioning. Neural messages are filtered through the feeling brain first, such that if a message is highly emotionally charged, the message may get hijacked and never make it to the frontal lobes for processing in the thinking part of the brain. If a message is short-circuited, the brain's response will be fright or flight. When this happens, the child cannot learn because messages are not making it to the rational part of the brain. This neurological fact points to the need for a stable environment in which children's emotions can be mediated through the sense of belongingness provided by being members of a learning community. Their inclusion in the learning community is reinforced when their photos are displayed. However, the mere presence of photos does not guarantee that emotions will always be stable.

Goleman (1995) posits that knowing one's emotions is the first step in bypassing the emotional filter and allowing messages to proceed for rational processing. "Self-awareness—recognizing a feeling as it happens—is the keystone of emotional intelligence" (Goleman, p. 43). Since developmentally appropriate practice not only focuses on academics but also strives to teach the "whole child," opportunities present themselves for teachers to address emotional development as one curricular area. According to the draft of the 2008 revision of the National Association for the Education of Young Children's (NAEYC) *Position Statement on Developmentally Appropriate Practice,* the concept of the "whole child" is addressed as one of the principles of child development and learning that inform practice. "All the domains of development and learning—physical, social, emotional, and cognitive—are important, and they are closely interrelated. Children's development and learning in one domain influence and are influenced by what takes place in other domains" (p. 15). Therefore, all areas of development (cognitive, language, fine and large motor, social, emotional, creative, and cultural awareness) are connected.

Educators teach children about their emotions by addressing the social/emotional domain of development when teaching the whole child. Children who are identified to be on the autism spectrum particularly benefit from activities that help them to discern emotions and emotional facial expressions. Children learn to identify feelings by looking at other children's expressions, as in "Look at Suzy—she has a sad face." Other methods that are employed to label emotions are to sing songs like "If You're Happy and You Know It, Sad and You Know It, Angry and You Know It . . ." with an emphasis on affect as the song is sung and animated. When singing such songs, photos of children expressing emotions, as shown in Figure 1.2, can be used to provide a model while the children sing. Another way that teachers address emotions is to have posters of children with different emotional expressions displayed in the room. Such posters would be more meaningful if photos of children's faces from that classroom were used to demonstrate the emotions.

Figure 1.2 Photos That Show Emotions

More examples of using photos to enhance emotional development will be presented in Chapter 8.

Goleman (1995) defines emotional intelligence (EI) as "being able to motivate oneself and persist in the face of frustrations; to control impulse and delay gratification; to regulate one's moods and keep distress from swamping the ability to think; to empathize and to hope" (p. 34). The development of EI is a process. Using digital photographs can assist educators as they guide children through the process of identifying emotions in a stable, inclusive environment in which the child belongs.

Erikson's Psychosocial Theory

Erik Erikson's (1963) theory offers dichotomies that represent the resolution of inner conflicts that people face in progressive stages of psychosocial development. His third stage of psychosocial development, which occurs in the preschool years, is concerned with the child's developing initiative rather than guilt. This theory is one of the foundations of the practice of offering developmentally appropriate choices to children during the preschool day.

Many early-learning environments actualize this part of Erikson's theory when a variety of learning centers are available to young children during large blocks of time, often called "choice time" or "centers time." To manage participation and still offer children choices, teachers have learned to limit the number of children participating in each center through the use of limit signs (the example in Figure 1.3 shows a sign that limits participation to two children). Some limit signs merely post the number that may participate in a center. Other limit signs may be pocket charts with limited spaces, such that children insert their nametags into

Figure 1.3   Limit Sign

pockets to signal their choices; when the pockets are full, children know to move to a different center. Another limit sign uses Velcro fasteners, such that children attach their nametags to the Velcro to signal their choices; again, when the spaces are filled on this Velcro chart, the children know to move to another learning center.

Since young children are in the process of learning to read their names, names are often paired with symbols so that the children can recognize them. For example, if Bethany knows that her name is always paired with the butterfly sticker, she can easily find her nametag and move it from chart to chart as she selects centers. With the use of digital images, the children's names can be paired with their photographs. This facilitates more meaningful learning, as the children recognize not only their images and names over time but also begin to "read" the names of every member of the class.

Vygotsky's Socio-Cultural Theory

Another theorist who has contributed to developmentally appropriate practices in early childhood education is Lev Vygotsky. Vygotsky's theory (1978) is concerned with a child's cognitive development within a society and a culture. He viewed play as one of the foundational activities for children's learning because it enhanced the child's imagination. Through play, children can reach potentials in their zones of proximal development. The zone of proximal development is Vygotsky's unique way of observing and assessing development. Instead of only assessing what a child can do independently, which Vygotsky viewed as the lower end of the zone of proximal development, he advocated for projecting what a child might do if assisted as being the higher end of the zone of proximal development. For example, a child might be assisted to learn by interaction with an adult or more competent peer or through the use of symbols as tools.

An application of Vygotsky's theory in the early learning environment would be to offer children choices to learn through play. Some of these choices might be structured in learning centers in which symbol systems, like digital photographs, that depict a sequence of steps to achieve an outcome guide children toward their upper limits of the zone of proximal development. Some activities in learning centers are structured toward specific outcomes. For example, if a teacher has designed a learning center in which a child is to prepare a snack independently, the teacher would task-analyze how to prepare the snack. Photos of those steps toward achievement can be posted in a process chart in a learning center. (See an example of a Cooking Center Process Chart in Chapter 10.) This process chart scaffolds the child's learning and guides the child to success. The photos serve as mediators. Achievement of the desired outcome is fostered when the children can "read" the step-by-step photo directions and independently navigate their personal zones of proximal development while gaining skills. Process charts are useful in centers such as those for snack making, art, science, and math when a specific outcome is desired.

Piaget's Stages of Cognitive Development

Jean Piaget (1952) has long been recognized as a theorist who greatly influenced developmentally appropriate practices in early childhood education. His cognitive stage theory demonstrated that young children learn differently than older children. In the early years, children learn through their senses and through interaction with objects. The preschool child is primarily in Piaget's preoperational stage. "Egocentric behavior is probably the most striking characteristic of the preoperational child" (Singer & Revenson, 1996, p. 34). Egocentric children see things from their points of reference and cannot take on other's perceptions of a situation.

Because egocentric children focus on themselves, using photos of children takes advantage of that egocentrism to turn their focus toward other learning. For example, if a child's photo appears in a book, the child is more likely to be motivated to read that book. If a child's photo is part of a game, the child will be drawn to that game. Making children part of the curriculum by including photos of them in curriculum materials or books contributes to the meaningfulness of the materials. Imagine children putting together puzzles of themselves and being challenged by the complexity and number of pieces involved to organize a completed picture (see Figure 1.4). Because the completed picture results in seeing their own images, the children are motivated to persevere at the task.

Montessori: The Montessori Method

Maria Montessori (1964), like Erikson, wanted to encourage independence in children. She advocated for children to have "liberty"; that is, to be able to move about the classroom self-selecting activities in which to become engaged. She stated, "The first, active manifestations of the child's individual liberty must be so guided that through this activity he may arrive at independence" (pp. 95–96). One of her areas of concentration was that of "practical life" in which children learned self-help skills related to personal cleanliness, environmental cleanliness, and cooking skills. To teach these skills, a teacher might task analyze the skill and present the skill as a series of steps via photos. Thus, practical life skills are developed using digital photography as a guide to task completion. An example using photography to

Figure 1.4   Puzzle

develop a life skill is a hand-washing chart (see Chapter 7) by a sink that would guide the child through the steps in proper hand washing. Similarly, photo charts of skills could be developed to demonstrate steps in shoe tying, carrot grating, or floor sweeping.

Bruner's Mentalities

Jerome Bruner is a cognitive theorist who looks at icons or images as one of three pathways to learning. He addresses three types of learning, which he refers to as *mentalities.* He "structures cognitive abilities into a set of mentalities. The three main areas are the enactive, the iconic, and the symbolic mentality" (www.mprove.de/diplom/text/3.2.2_three stages.html).

The enactive mentality parallels Piaget's sensory-motor stage of development, when a child learns by doing, by manipulating three-dimensional objects, and by experiencing through the senses. The second phase, the iconic phase, occurs after the toddler stage and continues on through the primary grades or until about age eight. In this phase, the child depends upon icons or pictures to learn and think. Since photographic images are icons, Bruner's theory, like Vygotsky's theory, would support the use of photos to guide children's learning during the preschool and primary years.

Gardner's Multiple Intelligences

Howard Gardner (1983) posits that humans have many ways of learning and knowing. The personal intelligences, interpersonal intelligence and intrapersonal intelligence, are concerned with cognitively knowing about feelings and moods related to others and to oneself. Gardner as cited in Goleman (1995) offers these summaries of definitions of these intelligences:

> Interpersonal intelligence is the ability to understand other people; what motivates them, how they work, how to work cooperatively with them. . . . Interpersonal intelligence . . . is a correlative ability, turned inward. It is a capacity to form an accurate, veridical model of oneself and to be able to use that model to operate effectively in life. (p. 39)

When children can see themselves at the center of learning materials, intrapersonal intelligence is fostered. Seeing one's own image assists one in reflecting about the photo. In addition, when a child can see images of others in curriculum materials, interpersonal intelligence is fostered as the child thinks about the images of others. When curriculum materials include photos of children expressing various emotions, these two types of intelligence are addressed.

Gagné's Conditions of Learning

The conditions of learning theory, developed by Robert Gagné (1985), recognizes that learners have several types, or levels, of learning. Each type of learning requires a specific type of instructional method. According to Gagné's theory, there are five types of learning: verbal information, intellectual skills, cognitive strategies, motor skills, and attitudes. Both internal and external conditions are necessary for each type of learning.

The conditions of learning theory identifies nine instructional events with corresponding cognitive processes, which are intended to serve as a basis for designing instruction and selecting media, including digital photography (Gagné, Briggs, & Wager; 1992). The nine events of instruction, along with their cognitive processes (in parenthesis), are as follows:

1. Gaining the learner's attention (Reception)

2. Informing learners of the instructional objective (Expectancy)

3. Simulating recall of prior learning (Retrieval)

4. Presenting stimulus (Selective Perception)

5. Providing learning guidance (Semantic Encoding)

6. Eliciting performance (Responding)

7. Providing feedback (Reinforcement)

8. Assessing performance (Retrieval)

9. Enhancing retention and transfer (Generalization)

Table 1.2 shows an example that illustrates how a teacher may sequence instruction corresponding to the nine events when teaching students to recognize the sounds of the letter *A*.

For early childhood educators, the nine events of instruction can provide a road map to integrate digital photography at various stages of

Table 1.2 Sequencing Instruction Using the Nine Events of Instruction

Nine Events of Instruction	Cognitive Process and Instructional Strategy
1. Gaining the learner's attention	(Reception): Show a bag with the letter *A* printed on it.
2. Informing learners of the instructional objective	(Expectancy): Present the question "What starts with the sounds that the letter *A* makes?"
3. Simulating recall of prior learning	(Retrieval): Review the sounds of the letter *A*.
4. Presenting stimulus	(Selective Perceptions): Provide an illustration: *apple* starts with the short *A* sound; *ape* starts with the long *A* sound.
5. Providing learning guidance	(Semantic Encoding): Have children reach into bag and withdraw an object that starts with an *A* sound.
6. Eliciting performance	(Responding): Ask learners if the object starts with a short *A* or long *A* sound.
7. Providing feedback	(Reinforcement): Reinforce correct responses; redirect incorrect responses.
8. Assessing performance	(Retrieval): Place objects in categories of short *A* or long *A* sounds.
9. Enhancing retention and transfer	(Generalization): Show photos of objects and ask learners to identify which have short *A* or long *A* sounds.

SOURCE: Courtesy of Linda Good and John Solis. Used with permission.

instruction. Gagné's nine events of instruction illustrate that instructional goals and objectives guide what specific instructional technology and media, including digital photography, are appropriate to support learning and the instructional process.

Keller's Motivational Model

In today's classroom, students' motivation to learn significantly impacts how teachers prepare the learning environment and deliver instruction to optimize student learning. John Keller (1983, 1987) developed the ARCS motivational model, which attempted to guide educators in promoting and sustaining learner motivation. ARCS is an acronym that represents four specific areas that contribute to a learner's motivation to learn: attention, relevance, confidence, and satisfaction.

Attention

Effective classroom instructional strategies capture students' curiosity and interests. Attention also helps to eliminate boredom in the classroom. Teachers should also keep in mind that many students are not only auditory or visual learners but are multisensory learners (Shelly, Cashman, Gunter, & Gunter, 2006). Integrating digital media into lesson plans can gain students' attention by accommodating a variety of learning styles. Lessons that aim to capture students' attention use a variety of instructional techniques, such as visual aids, stories, thought-provoking questions, short lectures, and small discussion groups. Digital photography, for example, can be used to tell stories, illustrate real-world objects to which students can relate, and help learners understand complex ideas.

Relevance

Much of student motivation can be attributed to students' feeling that learning is important to their lives. Lessons that feel relevant to the learner not only emphasize the meaningfulness of current skills but also their connection to previously learned skills. Instructional strategies that could promote relevance in classroom lessons include telling learners how new skills will build on previously learned skills, explaining what the new skills will do for the learners today, and explaining what the new skills will do for the learners in the future.

Confidence

Students often achieve learning when they believe they can. Digital media, including digital photography, can be used in lessons that challenge different skill levels, promote positive expectations, and provide learner feedback. Individual learners need to feel that if they exert their own efforts toward a challenge (i.e., a specific instructional objective), they are capable of achievement. Ultimately, classroom objectives should be matched to a student's skill level and abilities. Such lessons set the foundation for students to achieve success and acquire confidence in their own ability to learn.

Satisfaction

Learning needs to be rewarding or satisfying in some way, such as giving the student a sense of self-achievement, garnering positive feedback from authoritative figures, or being entertaining. Learners should feel as though newly acquired skills are useful by being provided opportunities to use the new skills in real settings. Digital photography, for example, can be used with students to identify and relate to real-world objects, people, and places. Continuous feedback and reinforcement are needed to sustain a desired behavior. The most powerful reinforcement occurs when students find that a learning experience is relevant and useful to their own world or the one in which they aspire to live (Shelly et al., 2006).

Brain Research

Jane Healy (1990) expresses concern that we may be changing children's brains through the language and experiences to which we expose them. She states that "two variables—companionship and active involvement with toys—differentiate between 'enriched' and 'impoverished' conditions" for learning" (p. 70). Using photos does not preclude the use of appropriate language or the exclusion of developmentally appropriate experiences that encourage active engagement and peer interactions. In fact, the use of photos can contribute to an enriched condition for learning. When photos are used to guide a child to success in a learning center through a process chart, the child is actively involved in the activity; peers can relate to each other and the activity without direct adult instruction. Another example is when a teacher or peers serve as companions in exploring a book that includes photos of the children.

Healy (1990) further states that "any activity which engages a student's interest and imagination, which sparks the desire to seek out an answer, or ponder a question, or create a response, can be good potential brain food" (p. 73). When photos of children are included in the educational environment, children are motivated. For example, if the teacher creates a photo book based on the chant "Who Took the Cookies From the Cookie Jar?" children's interests are sparked as they wonder who will be featured on the next page. Children often respond to the story, either with the given response "Who me?" or with their own responses. Stories like this contribute to time spent listening to stories, because children often want to read them more than once. Healy reports on a study by Dr. Wells and his colleagues that found "the most powerful predictor of . . . school achievement was the amount of time spent listening to interesting stories" (p. 92). When photos are used to supplement language, but not to supplant it, an enriched environment develops.

Brain research has raised awareness that it is important to create associations that "link new learning to something that is personally relevant to the student" (Wolfe, 2001, p. 105). This is an effective way to make meaning and, therefore, build synapses in the brain. When digital photos of children are taken on a field trip and then incorporated into a class-made book about the field trip, the children are more likely to retain information about the field trip experience. Any time a teacher presents material in multiple ways, children are more likely to retain the information.

TEACHER STATEMENT 1

When I was a college student, I was working with young children with special needs and was teaching them the fingerplay *Five Little Monkeys Jumping on a Bed*. After being introduced to the fingerplay, I had the children act out the story with some simple props. While they were acting it out, I snapped photos of them with a digital camera. I then imported those photos into a PowerPoint presentation and printed off books—one large book for the classroom and smaller books for each child to take home. I also used a program called Pinnacle Studio to create a video presentation using the same photos. I imported music and added it to the same video. I burned the video to a DVD and brought it to school for the children to watch. The children were so excited to see themselves on TV. Many of them sang along and cheered as they saw their pictures. The video was a fantastic review of the previous day's lesson. Each child, after completing the lesson, was able to count backwards from five.

—Annie Tietz Kindergarten Teacher

SOURCE: Courtesy of Annie Tietz. Used with permission.

When children saw photos of themselves enacting the fingerplay, the material became personally relevant and meaningful, thus contributing to learning by strengthening synaptic connections.

Statements From Professional Organizations

NAEYC has published a position statement "Technology and Young Children—Ages 3 through 8" (www.naeyc.org/about/positions/PSTECH 98.asp). "Early childhood educators have a responsibility to . . . be prepared to use technology to benefit children" (¶ 2). This document lists seven issues related to using technology with young children:

- Evaluation
- Benefits
- Integration into the learning environment
- Equitable access to technology
- Software cautions with regards to stereotyping and violence
- The role of teachers and parents
- The implications for professional development

This document encourages the use of technology to integrate curriculum across subjects. It also focuses on teachers' needs for in-depth training and ongoing support so that technology can be appropriately and effectively used in early learning classrooms. The position statement also encourages the use of technology as a tool for communicating and collaborating among professionals as well as for teaching children. When teachers use a resource book, such as this one, they gain skills in expanding their use of digital cameras and see other uses for computer programs, such as PowerPoint.

NAEYC has established "Standards for Initial Licensure Programs: Early Childhood Professional Preparation" (www.naeyc.org/faculty/pdf/2001.pdf), which have also been approved by the National Council for Accreditation of Teacher Education (NCATE). "Technology has taken a central place in early childhood programs" ("Standards," p. 18). Teachers of young children are expected to be competent at integrating technology as a tool for teaching. "Appropriate technology, including . . . cameras . . . can support and expand young children's learning" (p. 18–19). Preservice training programs are preparing the teachers of tomorrow to use today's technology.

The International Society for Technology in Education (ISTE, 2000) has established standards for students from PreK through Grade 12 that connects curriculum and technology. Some of the standards for PreK through Grade 2 address using a variety of media and technology resources for developing learning activities; working cooperatively and collaboratively with others when using technology in the classroom; and creating developmentally appropriate multimedia products with support from teachers, family members, or student partners. Teachers must gain knowledge and skills to guide children in their skill development. When teachers model the appropriate use of digital cameras and computer programs to work with those digital images, young children can begin the process of gaining similar skills.

A Report From an Educational Organization

The Northwest Regional Educational Laboratory has published a report entitled "Technology in Early Childhood Education: Finding the Balance" (www.netc.org/earlyconnections/byrequest.html). This report links child development in five developmental domains to the impact of technology. While most of this report is related to computer usage, it does address digital cameras as tools to record students' activities while they are working, performing, or experiencing special events. For example, digital images on which children write or dictate captions can be used as aids in storytelling. The report notes that photos are a communication tool for sharing with other students, parents, or community members. It also notes that photos can be used to introduce teachers and staff members to new students and families during home visits. Examples of uses of digital images are given for a Head Start Program in Portland, Oregon.

Practical Reasons

One advantage of using digital imagery noted by Browne (2005/ 2006) is its immediacy: images can be seen within seconds on the LCD screen and can be downloaded to computers and printed within minutes. He also states that digital cameras have "stamina" (i.e., they don't run out of film). A third benefit is that teachers can review pictures immediately and delete unwanted photos. Because images are digital, computer software can be used to crop photos so that teachers become their own editors.

Other practical reasons for using digital photography relate to using images as communication strategies. Photos can be shared with staff, parents, and the media. Photos can provide documentation for conferences and can demonstrate children's abilities or illustrate any special needs they have.

Other Support for Using Digital Imagery

Pastor and Kerns (1997), two teachers in a kindergarten setting, report their observations and conclusions about using digital photography. They had children use digital cameras for photographing experiences on a field trip. After the field trip, the children wrote about the pictures.

Later, the children used the photos and their writing to communicate about their experiences to their parents. Another time, the children produced a photo book of a cooking experience. The final photographic project was the production of a slide show on HyperStudio at the end of the school year. Pastor and Kerns conclude:

> Digital photography, especially, plays an important role in the early childhood classroom for two reasons. First, it offers children a way to preserve and reproduce special moments for reflection— potent stimulus to writing. Second, teachers can use the selected moments for further discussion and possible curriculum expansion, as well as share classroom experiences with parents. (p. 45)

DeMarie (2001) reports how young children use cameras and what kinds of images they capture. When asked to take a picture of their favorite person in the room, young children photographed their teacher. When taking photos of a field trip to a zoo, young preschoolers took pictures of familiar animals or parts of animals rather than of zoo animals. The author stated: "Preschool children enjoyed common events focused on action and seemed to treat the camera like a set of binoculars for looking at things" ("Photographs and Words of Preschool Children Who Were 3 to 5 Years Old").

Cynthia Hoisington (2002) reports using photographs to support children's science inquiry when she taught a unit on building structures. She observed that the use of photos helped children persist in their building. The photos helped children to reflect on their building, thus reviewing materials and strategies. Photos were used to discuss and solve problems with building.

According to a research study by DeMarie and Ethridge (2006), when young children have access to cameras and take photos of their experiences, the photos can be used to enhance language development as children discuss the photos with their parents. DeMarie and Ethridge discovered that the use of photos enriched children's conversations. Allowing children to take photos also gave insights into what young children deem important—peer interactions and experiences. Although instamatic cameras were used in this study and children were limited to the twelve exposures in a roll of film, the principle of using photographic images would be transferable to digital images.

Anecdotal evidence also points to the value of using digital images for teaching a literacy lesson. A teacher in Hong Kong published a teacher-made children's book based on the nursery rhyme "Mary Had a Little Lamb" in which she used photos of children from her class and images of animals downloaded from the Internet paired with simple lines of patterned text. For example, one of the pages of the book read: "Ben had a little duck. Its feathers were as soft as cotton." The teacher reported that the children in her class typically had a difficult time attending to stories; however, using this book with their photos in it resulted in their listening very carefully. They became engaged in the book and in brainstorming more analogies, such as "feathers were as soft as a pillow," and they were motivated to have the story read to them multiple times.

When one consults the research base for statistically significant studies to support the use of technology in early childhood education, one finds a litany of articles related to computer use. However, few research studies cited at this time relate to the use of digital images and young children. There are articles related to how to select (Browne, 2005/2006; Park, 2002; Walker & Donohue, 2006a, 2006b) or use digital cameras or photographic images (DeMarie & Ethridge, 2006; Duncan, n.d.; Good, 2005/2006; Starr, 2002, 2004), and there are some books (Entz & Galarza, 2000; Geyer & Geyer, 2005; and Lawrence, 2005) on how to use digital cameras or photos in early childhood education. However, only a limited research base points to the benefits or deficits of using photographic images. The door to this line of research is wide open!

LOOKING BACK/LOOKING AHEAD

Part I has provided the foundation for why digital images are useful in early education. Part II consists of five chapters that prepare the teacher to acquire the tools necessary for implementing this form of technology in the classroom, as well as some tips for successful implementation. The reader will learn about hardware, software, consumables, permission forms, photography tips, record keeping, and organization and will be given some detailed guidance in implementing the PowerPoint program.

Part II

Lights, Camera, Action

Getting Started With Digital Photography in Your Classroom

One for the Money **2**

Hardware, Software, and
Consumables

Linda Good with John Solis

$\mathbf{A}$s you begin this new technological journey in your classroom, it is necessary to obtain hardware, software, and consumable materials. Some of the items mentioned below are obvious, but others require a bit of explaining to make clear their uses in digital photography. Table 2.1 offers a basic list.

HARDWARE

Digital Cameras

A digital camera captures and stores pictures digitally rather than on photographic film. Digital photos are stored on storage media devices and transferred to a computer for display or manipulation. (Storage media devices will be discussed later in this chapter.) There are three general categories of digital cameras based on cost, features, and image resolution: (a) point-and-shoot; (b) field, sometimes referred to as an advanced point-and-shoot camera; and (c) professional.

Point-and-shoot digital cameras require little to no adjustment before capturing a picture. Field, or advanced point-and-shoot, digital cameras provide added features, which allow a user to make manual adjustments and change lenses before capturing a picture to increase

AUTHOR'S NOTE: This chapter was written with the help of colleague John Solis, PhD (Technology Integration Specialist, Richland School District Two, Columbia, SC 29229).

Table 2.1   Checklist of Things You Need

Required Hardware:

___Digital camera, battery-charging unit, downloading cables or card reader

___Computer

___Printer or photo printer

Required Software:

___ Appropriate memory/storage unit

___ Program for downloading photos (often supplied with the camera or with your computer—for example, iPhoto on Macintosh computers)

___Microsoft PowerPoint or Microsoft Word programs on your computer

Note: The examples provided in this book are based on Microsoft Word 2003 and PowerPoint 2003 for a Mac OS X 2003 system; other versions of these programs used on other platforms may require some adjustments for your use.

Consumable Materials:

___Rechargeable batteries for camera

___Photo paper, although you can print on regular printer paper or other printable materials

___Appropriate printer cartridges

___CDs

___DVDs (if producing videos)

___Three-ring binders

___ Clear plastic sheet protectors

___Small photo albums

___ Clear contact paper or laminating machine

___ Magnetic tape rolls or magnetic paper

In addition to printing on paper or photo paper, a supply of self- adhesive labels, pellon (fabric used to line clothing), sheets of magnetic paper, and iron-on photo transfer sheets would be useful.

---

image quality. The professional digital camera provides users with greater control over exposure, lenses, color, and image resolution. So which camera should a teacher consider? Let's consider the three major variables for selecting a digital camera for classroom use: image resolution, camera features, and cost.

Image Resolution

Manufacturers describe the image resolution of digital cameras in terms of how many megapixels (millions of pixels) a camera can produce (Lever-Duffy & McDonald, 2008). A pixel (also known as a picture element) is simply a single dot in a picture captured by a digital camera. A single picture is made up of millions of dots. The more dots a digital camera can produce, the clearer the resulting picture, as shown in Table 2.2.

Table 2.2   Megapixels and Quality

Digital Camera's Megapixels Capability	Photo Quality and Print Size
2–3 megapixels	Produces good detailed computer screen photos, as well as excellent 4 × 6 inch and very good 5 × 7 inch prints. Some cameras may produce fair quality 8 × 10 prints.
4–5 megapixels	Produces images equivalent to 35 mm photo prints and high-quality 8 × 10 inch prints
6 or more megapixels	Allows user to crop and increase the size of a portion within a photo without losing clarity, and 8 × 10 inch or higher prints are high quality.

SOURCE: From Lever-Duffy, Judy, & McDonald, Jean B. *Teaching and Learning With Technology* (3rd ed.). Boston: Allyn & Bacon. Copyright © 2008 by Pearson Education. Reprinted by permission of the publisher.

The resolution range for most point-and-shoot digital cameras is five or fewer megapixels. As discussed later in this chapter, a camera's megapixel capability is directly correlated with cost. If a teacher has no need to print photos larger than 5 × 7 inches, then a two- to three-megapixel camera is ideal. Other point-and-shoot cameras are capable of capturing four- to five-megapixel images. Field and professional cameras are typically capable of capturing images at five or more megapixels.

Camera Features

When capturing photos with digital cameras, teachers should remember that all cameras, regardless of size, shape, brand, or type, operate on the same basic principles (Smaldino, Lowther, & Russell, 2008). Light reflects off the subject and passes through the camera lens to form an image on storage media. However, teachers should consider certain basic features of digital cameras when selecting a camera.

- *Flash:* All digital cameras have a shutter button that allows light to enter the camera through the lens to capture a photograph. A flash provides extra light when capturing pictures in dark or ill-lit areas. Most digital cameras have additional buttons or settings that allow the user to control the flash feature.
- *Zoom:* A zoom feature allows a user to bring the image of a subject closer to the viewing area to capture as a photograph.
- *Battery format:* Many of today's digital cameras use AA batteries, which are easy for teachers to swap out when it is time for new batteries. The ideal camera has a long battery life or uses rechargeable batteries.
- *LCD screen:* An LCD screen can be used for three purposes: as an image viewer when capturing photos, as a photo slide viewer to determine if a photo should be deleted from the camera's memory or not, and as a photo viewer to determine if another photo of the same activity should be taken.
- *Video out:* Although it is not always necessary, most of today's digital cameras have a video out feature. The video out feature allows a teacher to display photos from the camera's internal or external storage media on a display monitor, projector, or any display device that can receive a video signal. In most cases, a digital camera can function as a photo "slide presentation" device through the video out feature.
- *Storage media and expansion slots:* Most digital cameras have built-in storage media; however, this storage capacity is sometimes small, limiting the number of high-resolution images a teacher can save. Expansion slots give users the option to add external storage media memory cards, such as compact flash and Secure Digital (SD) cards, to save more photos.
- *More features:* Other features of today's digital cameras include menu options, photo slide viewer, delete option, delayed timer, and red-eye reduction. Image stabilization is a desirable feature that helps users avoid blurred images.

When selecting a camera for the children to use, the size, weight, and arrangement of the camera controls should be taken into account. Simplicity and ease in using are important considerations.

Specific features of point-and-shoot, field, and professional cameras vary by manufacturer and model. Support resources will be provided later in this chapter so that teachers can compare various types of cameras and their features.

Cost

One of the most important variables to consider when selecting a digital camera is cost. The cost of a digital camera depends primarily on the degree of image resolution and number of features. Cameras with higher megapixel capacities and added features are higher in price. Traditionally, the cost of electronics goes down over time as quality goes up, but you may regret waiting to purchase a digital camera. Because digital cameras have been around for a few years, good-quality cameras are now available at reasonable prices. As illustrated in Table 2.3, image resolution and features directly impact camera price.

Table 2.3   Resolution, Features, and Cost of Digital Cameras

Camera Type	Image Resolution Range	Camera Features	Cost Range
Point-and-shoot	Six megapixels or less	Fully automatic when turned on, easy to use, fits in a pocket, ideal for average consumer usage	Up to $600
Field, advanced point-and-shoot	Five megapixels or more	Portable yet flexible with the ability to change lenses and use other attachments, high level of control over exposure and added camera settings	$800 to $2,000
Professional	Five megapixels or more	Typically used for professional photography work, flexible with the widest range of lenses and added camera features/settings	$1,500 or more

SOURCE: From Shelly/Cashman/Gunter, *Teachers Discovering Computers: Integrating Technology and Digital Media in the Classroom, Fourth Edition*, 4E. © 2008 South-Western, a part of Cengage Learning, Inc. Reproduced by permission. www.cengage.com/permissions

Many of today's high-end point-and-shoot digital cameras are comparable to field cameras in quality and price. Most teachers will not want professional cameras for classroom use due to cost, classroom needs, and ease of use.

Selecting a Digital Camera

There are a number of questions that teachers need to consider when selecting a camera for classroom use.

1. Do I need to be able to print large and/or small photos?

2. Will I primarily be using the photos in a digital format (e.g., on Web sites, for computer activities, in PowerPoint presentations)?

3. Is the camera easy to use?

4. Do I need advanced features on the camera?

For most teachers, a two- to three-megapixel point-and-shoot camera is ideal if they will not need to print photos larger than 5 × 7 inches. Photos taken with cameras with two- to three-megapixel settings result in good-quality photos in a digital format for displaying on devices such as a computer screen, projector, or PowerPoint presentation. In addition, digital cameras in the two- to three-megapixel range are typically lower in cost and much easier to use than field, or professional, cameras, given the latter cameras' added features. If teachers need to print larger photos, 8 × 10 inches or larger, then a camera of more than three megapixels may be necessary. An image stabilization feature will aid in avoiding blurred images. Selecting a digital camera for classroom use is challenging, because teachers need to balance acceptable image quality or resolution with reasonable cost.

Settings for Capturing Images

Most of today's digital cameras have at least three image quality and size settings for capturing photos: low, standard, and fine. The setting used impacts photo file size and resolution. For sharing digital photos via e-mail or for Web page development, the low setting is ideal, generating small file sizes and enough resolution for computer viewing. The recommended resolution setting for photos to be sent over e-mail is 640 × 480 pixels.

The standard setting is ideal for high-quality photos for Web sites and other electronic documents. Photos taken at the standard setting can be sent through e-mail, but larger file sizes can increase download time for photo files. In addition, photos taken at the standard setting are ideal for printing as 4 × 6 inch pictures.

Photos taken at the fine setting are ideal for printing large, high-quality photographs. However, fine photos are not ideal for e-mail or for Web site development, as the larger file size can significantly increase download time.

Specific photo sizes and resolutions for low, standard , and fine settings vary depending on the camera.

Many digital cameras give the user the option to choose a photo, or image, file format. The two most common file formats are Tagged Image File Format (TIFF) and Joint Photographic Experts Group (JPEG). Saving files in TIFF format typically results in large files, meaning that only few images can be stored on storage media, but the photos are normally high quality. Saving files in JPEG format results in some quality degradation, but the files are smaller.

Saving Images to Storage Media

A digital camera stores photos on either internal storage media built into the camera, reusable storage memory cards, or miniature hard drives or DVDs. Reusable memory cards include compact flash, Secure Digital (SD), and Microdrives. A teacher can assume that the storage media that comes with a newly purchased digital camera is of low capacity and may be inadequate for storing a large number of photos. What type of storage media a teacher chooses to expand on the camera's built-in storage depends on the camera's capabilities.

Storage media have various capacities for saving large numbers of photos and high-resolution photos. Photos' storage on internal and/or external storage media should be temporary. When the storage device is full, photos can be transferred to more permanent storage, such as a computer's hard drive or network folder. Photos from some storage media can be downloaded into a computer by inserting the storage media card into a slot on the computer; other systems require connecting the camera to a computer port with a USB 2.0 or Firewire cable to download photos.

Printers

Once digital photographs have been captured, they are ready to be printed, if desired, for classroom use. Classroom teachers typically print digital photos on a color printer (but may choose the black-and-white print option) or send them to a professional service. In either case, a teacher should capture photos at resolutions high enough for various print sizes.

A printer is an output device that produces text and graphics on a physical medium, such as paper or transparency sheets (Shelly et al., 2006). Print quality is measured in dots per inch (dpi). The higher the dpi capability of a printer, the higher the quality of the printed photograph. Printer manufacturers offer printers with different speeds, capabilities, and printing methods to meet teachers' various print requirements. Until a few years ago, printing documents required connecting a printer to a computer through the use of a USB or parallel port cable, but today printing can often be accomplished by placing a camera on a printer docking station, directly connecting the camera to the printer via USB cable, inserting media cards directly to a printer, and wireless printing via IrDA ports or Bluetooth technology.

Printers suitable for digital photography are ink-jet printers, photo printers, and laser printers. Ink-jet printers spray small drops of ink (black and/or color) onto paper. Ink-jets normally produce high-quality graphics and text while being relatively inexpensive. Photo printers are color printers designed to produce professional-quality photo prints.

Photo printers typically use ink-jet technology to produce photo prints of various sizes. A laser printer is a high-speed printer that utilizes a laser beam to produce text and graphics. The laser beam alters an electrical charge on a drum. This drum is then rolled through a reservoir of powdered ink, referred to as toner. Toner is picked up by the electrical charges on the drum and finally transferred onto paper through the combination of heat and pressure. Laser printers print high-quality black-and-white graphics and text quickly.

A major consideration when selecting a printer is the future cost required to keep it supplied with ink or toner cartridges.

Selecting a Printer

Selecting a printer to print digital photographs for classroom use requires balancing cost, features, and print quality. Most teachers choose between ink-jet and laser printers. Color ink-jet printers may cost from $50 to $300 on average. Common laser printers may cost from $200 to $2,000 on average. As a general rule, the cheaper the printer, the lower the print quality and speed and the more often ink or toner cartridges have to be replaced. Laser printers are fast with greater print quality but are more expensive. If color is desirable, a teacher should use a high-end ink-jet printer to ensure quality. To print color photos, teachers should use a photo printer or high-end ink-jet printer rather than a laser printer. Because printing in color is costly, the user can select to print in black-and-white when in the PowerPoint Print function.

Computer System

The computer system is an important hardware component that allows teachers and students to share, manage, print, manipulate, and integrate digital photographs into specific classroom activities. The computer system displays, stores, and transfers digital photos to a printer or to use in other electronic formats, such as PowerPoint presentations or Web sites. A computer should have an adequate amount of memory and storage capacity to handle the large amounts of data contained in high-resolution digital photographs. In addition, a computer should have high-speed interfaces to a digital camera and printer along with a fast central processing unit (CPU) to control digital photo processing functions. Table 2.4 lays out a recommended computer system configuration for digital photography.

Today's Windows-based and Macintosh-based computer systems are all adequate for basic digital photography and should not be a major

Table 2.4   Recommended Computer System Configuration for Digital
Photography

Minimum Recommended Computer System Requirements
• Processor (CPU) speed: 1.4 GHz or higher
• Random access memory (RAM): 128 MB
• Hard drive capacity: 80 GB or higher
• Interface: USB 2.0 or Firewire ports (check what the digital camera uses)
• Standard display monitor
• Windows or Macintosh operating systems

SOURCE: Courtesy of John Solis. Used with permission.

concern in determining which computer system to use. Teachers may
simply need to determine if an assigned computer system is sufficient for
digital photography.

Scanners

If you don't want to take photos of 35 mm pictures or student work or
other documents, a device to consider buying is a scanner. A scanner is
not essential (such devices are termed "peripheral"), but it can be used to
create electronic versions of print-based instructional materials, such as
student drawings, 35 mm photographs, and other documents. Scanned
images can be integrated into PowerPoint presentations, word processor
documents, and other educational applications. In general, images
scanned at any resolution will maintain their original quality when a user
manually decreases the size for print or computer use, but quality is lost
when the digital version of an image is manually increased in size.

Today's scanners fall into three category types: flatbed, document,
and hand-held. For typical classroom use, the flatbed scanner is an ideal
option. Flatbed scanners look like the top of a copy machine with a large
glass plate on which to place documents, images, or another object to be
scanned. A user simply lifts the lid of the flatbed scanner and places the
document or object facedown on the glass plate. The software that comes
with the scanner will normally control the device and provide users with
basic photo/document/object editing. A recommended cost for a suitable
scanner is $200 or less.

Support Resources

Selecting the hardware necessary to capture, store, share, and print digital photos can be a time-consuming task. When purchasing hardware for digital photography, it is a good idea for teachers to take some time to research various hardware resources to balance cost, quality, ease of use, and, most importantly, classroom needs. Table 2.5 provides teachers with resources to get a good start in comparing hardware resources for digital photography classroom integration.

The resources identified in Table 2.5 provide teachers with a start on making decisions about the appropriate hardware necessary for digital imaging and photography. Teachers are highly encouraged to conduct their own research when comparing prices, quality, the center's or school's budget for technology, availability of hardware, and features of digital photography hardware before purchasing.

SOFTWARE

Software Applications

Once images are stored on a computer, digital imaging software allows teachers to share, manipulate, and integrate digital photographs to enhance both instructional practice and student learning. There are four general types of digital imaging software: editing, image management, presentation graphics, and creativity. Teachers should keep in mind that most hardware components, including a computer system, are normally accompanied by easy-to-use digital imaging software.

Editing Images

The power to manipulate digital photos can have positive implications for classroom instruction. Manipulating images may range from cropping and rotating to adjusting brightness and removing red-eye. Image editing software allows a user to alter and enhance digital images, as well as add special effects. The following is a list of common image editing modifications:

- Removing or reducing red-eye
- Adjusting brightness and contrast
- Rotating and flipping the picture's orientation
- Replacing original colors with new colors
- Cropping
- Adding text, icons, logos, and other visual elements
- Introducing special effects such as bevel, texture, and blurring

Table 2.5   Resources

Digital Cameras

- Digital Camera Resource Page
  www.dcresource.com—The Digital Camera Resource Page provides valuable resources such as a buyer's guide, price comparisons, and reviews of digital cameras.
- Short Courses
  www.shortcourses.com—From purchasing and using a digital camera to editing and taking nature photographs, this Web site contains a number of short courses on various digital camera topics.
- DigitalCameraInfo.com
  www.digitalcamerainfo.com—Compare prices and view user reviews of today's popular digital cameras by several manufacturers.

Storage Media

- Storage Card
  www.dpreview.com/learn/?/Glossary/Camera_System/storage_card_01.htm—This article, by Vincent Bockaert, describes the common types of removable storage media for digital cameras.
- Digital Camera Buyer's Guide
  www.epinions.com/buyers_guide/Digital_Cameras_buyers_guide_p1.html—It is a good idea to know how many pictures, on average, can be stored on a single storage media card at various image resolutions. You will find additional information on purchasing digital cameras as well.

Printers

- Printers: ZDNet Reviews
  http://review.zdnet.com/4566-3155_16-0.html—This guide allows the user to sort by price and product and read user reviews.

Computer Systems

- PC Buyer's Guide for Photography Fans
  www.microsoft.com/windowsxp/using/digitalphotography/getstarted/newPC.mspx—Although this guide focuses on the computers running the Windows operating system, the same concepts are applicable if considering a Macintosh system.
- Choosing a Computer System for Digital Imaging
  http://photo.net/equipment/digital/computers/—By Darron Spohn, this is another great resource for teachers who are considering utilizing a computer system for various digital imaging and photography tasks, such as photo editing, management, and sharing for classroom use.

Scanners

- Scanners: Buyer's Guide
  www.buyerzone.com/computers/scanners/buyers_guide1.html—Another useful guide for selecting a digital scanner for classroom use, this resource provides in-depth information on scanner types, features, resolution, and price.
- *PC World* Buyer's Guide to Scanners
  www.pcworld.com/article/id,102514-page,2-c,scanners/article.html—This article, by Rebecca Freed, is an easy-to-follow guide on scanner features and links that compares prices of common scanners used today.

Common applications for digital photo editing include Macromedia Fireworks and Josc Paint Shop Pro. More complex applications, such as Adobe Photoshop and Macromedia Fireworks, may cost between $100 and $650. However, most digital cameras, scanners, and some printers come with their own photo editing software that allows basic, easy-to-follow image editing.

Managing Images

It does not take long to become overwhelmed by a large quantity of digital photographs. Oftentimes, digital cameras do not save photographs with descriptive JPEG or TIFF file names. A variety of software tools, known as image management software, can help teachers identify, organize, and distribute digital photos. Computer hard disks and file folders can be scanned quickly to catalogue and organize photos, generate photo information, and sometimes edit digital photos.

Software tools such as Microsoft Office Picture Manager (see the screen shot in Figure 2.1) makes organizing digital photos an easy task. Microsoft Office Picture Manager offers basic digital photo editing tools. These tools include brightness and contrast adjustments, color adjustments, cropping, rotation and flipping, red-eye removal, image resizing, and picture compression. This software application also allows users to organize and rename photos stored on a PC; e-mail photographs to share with others; and view thumbnails, or small images, of the photos. Thumbnails can be located on a PC by double-clicking on the folder that contains the photo files, clicking on the View menu option, and then selecting the Thumbnails option.

Figure 2.1 Microsoft Office Picture Manager

Another image management software application commonly used by teachers is iPhoto, which is available on Macintosh computers. iPhoto presents photos as an array of thumbnails. To edit in iPhoto, either click on the image to be edited until it is highlighted and then click on the Edit button within the iPhoto program, or double-click on the image and the Edit function will open. Editing tools include cropping, red-eye reduction, enhancing, retouching, transforming to black-and-white, and adjusting brightness and contrast.

Other common image management software applications include Adobe Photo Album, ACDSee, and Image Fox. Many image managing software programs, such as those that come with digital cameras, scanners, and sometimes printers, have built-in photo editing tools. Teachers should check their Windows or Macintosh computer to determine if image management software is already installed. To view and evaluate a number of image management software applications, visit resources such as About.com at http://graphicssoft.about.com/od/imagemanagement/Image_Management_Image_Viewers_Organizers_Databases.htm and Imaging Resource at www.imaging-resource.com/SOFT.HTM or specific vendor Web sites.

Presentation Graphics Applications

At some point, teachers may decide to utilize digital photos through a digital medium to support specific instructional units or lessons. Tools that allow the creation of presentations to communicate ideas, messages, and other information to a specific target audience, such as students, are known as presentation graphics software (Shelly et al., 2006).

A common presentation graphics software application used by educators is Microsoft PowerPoint (see screen shot in Figure 2.2). Microsoft PowerPoint allows teachers and students to utilize multimedia such as graphics, video, audio, animation, and text to communicate ideas and create interactivity in the preK–12 classroom. Another common presentation graphics application in preK–12 schools is HyperStudio. HyperStudio is a multimedia authoring application that allows teachers to combine elements (e.g., text, graphics, video, animation, and audio) to create multimedia tools for interactive learning. Other common presentation graphics software applications in school settings include AppleWorks and Claris Works.

Presentation graphics software applications are typically used to create presentations in the form of slides that can be used to create overhead transparencies or printed handouts or books, as well as to present information in electronic form. This type of software application is important for educators, because electronic presentations can be integrated into

Figure 2.2   Microsoft PowerPoint Presentation Graphics

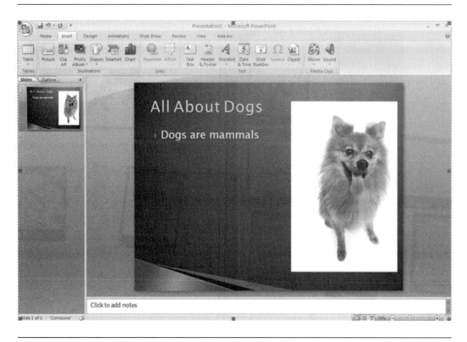

SOURCE: Courtesy of John Solis. Used with permission.

units or lessons. Teachers need to check the personal computers in their classrooms or consult with their schools' media specialists on the availability of presentation graphics software applications.

Creativity Software Applications

Other types of software applications can be used by teachers to integrate digital photos to support student learning. Creativity software, for example, is designed to allow students to display their own ideas through imagination and ingenuity. Students can control what multimedia elements, such as digital photos, are displayed using tools provided by the specific application. One popular creativity software application used in preK–5 settings is Kidspiration (see screen shot in Figure 2.3). When using Kidspiration, low-resolution, or e-mail-size, photos should be used so several pictures can be included in a project.

With Kidspiration, students can create customized image organizers by utilizing pictures, text, and audio to represent their ideas. Younger children can enhance their literacy and comprehension skills. Other creativity software applications that can integrate digital photography include Jump Start Artist, Kid Pix, Inspiration, Disney's Magic Artist, KidWorks, and iLife.

Figure 2.3   Kidspiration

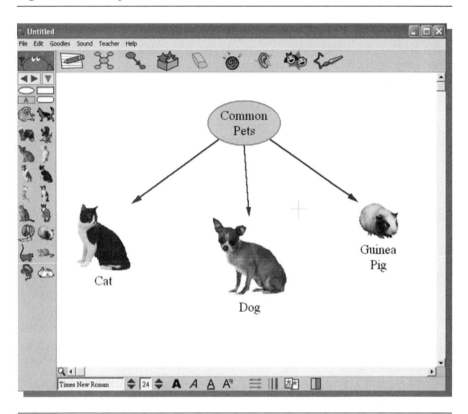

SOURCE: Courtesy of John Solis. Used with permission.

Other Applications

Early childhood teachers can utilize numerous software application tools to integrate digital photography into their teaching and enhance student learning. The selection of applications, particularly for presenting photos and having students interact with photos through creativity software, depends on several variables, including, but not limited to, student entry-level skills and capabilities, student learning styles, availability of software applications, and curriculum goals and objectives. Web site applications, such as Macromedia Dreamweaver, can be used to create Web-based learning activities, such as WebQuests, which can utilize digital photos but may not be age-appropriate for early childhood learners. Effective integration of digital photography to support teaching and learning depends on the needs of learners and identified curriculum goals and objectives. If no connection exists between curriculum goals/objectives and digital photos, teachers potentially waste valuable time for instruction.

CONSUMABLE MATERIALS

Once an investment has been made in hardware and software, consumables must be purchased and replenished to print the images. While some materials, like batteries, can be recharged, others get consumed and need to be restocked. Printer cartridges and paper or other print materials can be costly if used frequently and can strain anyone's budget. To alleviate out-of-pocket expenses, teachers might creatively seek ways to obtain consumable materials. Teachers might add some of the items to the students' required back-to-school supplies, such as requesting that students provide one of the following: printer cartridges (be sure to state brand, colors desired), photo paper, photo albums, etc. Parents might be asked to contribute supplies in lieu of birthday treats. Teachers can submit a wish list of consumables to the parent/teacher organization. As administrators become more aware of the value of using digital tools, they might add related materials to their supply budgets.

Teachers can also seek supply donations from discount department stores. For example, some large discount department stores have a donation application form available for nonprofit organizations. Others might have a matching grant application and permit public schools to do fundraising outside their stores to raise the matching money. Store chains that sell electronics and appliances have store donation fund applications, which focus on funding for nonprofit organizations that serve youth. Some office product stores have point clubs and/or offer discounts to teachers. Office supply stores that sell photographic paper and printer cartridges also have funds available. So be bold: ask!

Teachers can also request donations via Web sites set up expressly for this purpose. Two such sites are www.iloveschools.com and www.theteacherswishlist.com. Putting *donations teachers* into an Internet search engine will turn up many options.

Printer Cartridges

The available printer will require specific types of cartridges. Always make sure that a spare set of cartridges is available so that once a project is in process, it can be completed without running to the store to purchase more cartridges.

Printing Supplies: Paper

The quality of the printed matter depends on the quality of the paper. Although printing on photo paper is most desirable, it is also most expensive. An array of photo paper options is available, from good-quality paper for everyday printing use to professional-quality paper, from photo-sized paper to standard 8 1/2 × 11 inch sheets. To use a PowerPoint application, as this book does, it is best to purchase standard-sized sheets of photo paper. Personal preferences will dictate whether a matte or glossy finish is chosen. One can also print on typical computer paper, especially when making multiple copies for a number of children or families, but the quality is not as good.

Printing Supplies: Labels

Self-adhesive name badge labels or address-sized labels are available in office supply stores. Directions for formatting and printing tips are included within the packages. Photos can be printed on the labels along with the child's name. Photo labels are useful for many things, including labeling each child's folder or homework booklet, labeling the same message to be sent home for each child in the class, and personalizing a report to be shared with parents.

Printing Supplies: Pellon

Pellon is a translucent fabric that can be purchased in fabric stores or in fabric departments within discount department stores. It comes in a variety of textures. For tracing or printing purposes, a firmer, stiffer pellon is preferable so that it can be fed through a printer. Outlines of pictures can be traced onto pellon, colored with indelible markers, and cut out. The new twist is to print photos on pellon. Pellon sticks to flannel, so it is a desirable fabric to use to create flannelboard stories. Another use of pellon is to create a quilt for a fundraiser that has as its squares photos of children at school doing various projects or celebrating various events. Pellon is typically sold by the yard and does not come in a standard 8 1/2 × 11 inch paper, but it can be cut to paper size to be placed in the printer tray.

Printing Supplies: Magnetic Paper

Magnetic paper can be purchased in sheets or in name tag sizes from office supply stores, but it is expensive, so be selective as to when to print on magnetic paper. Photos can be printed on this special paper. Teachers can use magnetic boards, cookie sheets, or the backs of metal file cabinets as the showcase for these photo magnets to tell stories or for children to place their photos on upon arrival for attendance taking. Another use of magnetic paper is for puzzles. Imagine the delight on children's faces when they put together a puzzle of themselves!

Printing Supplies: Fabric

Iron-on photo transfer paper is available in office supply stores. Directions are included within the package for printing and then attaching the image to a T-shirt or other fabric with an ironing process. If parents will donate new, clean white or light-colored T-shirts and contribute a minimal amount for the iron-on transfer paper and printing costs, the teacher can supply each child with a T-shirt with a class photo. Inexpensive T-shirts are often available in craft stores.

Clear Contact Paper, Laminating, and Magnetic Strips

Because moisture or drips can damage ink-jet photos, it is critical to protect the photos when they are used in an interactive way. Cover the photo print with clear contact paper (available at discount stores in the housewares department) or laminate it. Self-adhesive magnetic tape (available at discount stores or hobby shops in the crafts department) placed on the back of laminated photos makes the photos part of your magnetic stories materials, or they can be used for a variety of charts when graphing in math and science activities. These types of activities will be explained and shown in Chapters 9 and 10.

Compact Disks

Compact disks (CDs) are a way to store your photos or slide shows and distribute them to parents. There are two types of CDs available. CD-Rs are one-use CDs; once you burn them, they cannot be written over again and revised. CD-RWs are read/write compact disks that can be used repeatedly. You can publicize your program by giving prospective consumers of your services a CD. The CD could contain a preview of the daily schedule or typical special events throughout the school year. At the end of the school year or for a special event gift (holidays, children's birthdays, at the conclusion of a child's week of being the Very Important Kid or Star of the Week), you can produce a slide show of photos of the children at school doing their favorite things, playing with their friends, and participating in activities. Burning a photo slideshow to a CD takes just minutes and strengthens the teacher/parent partnership. (Caution: Burning one CD takes minutes, but burning CDs for each family takes hours.)

Three-Ring Binders, Sheet Protectors, and Photo Albums

Children love to look at pictures of themselves, their friends, their field trips, their surroundings, and other special events in their lives at school. However, children are not always gentle with photos, so the photos need to be protected. A book that is produced by inserting photos in sheet protectors and then inserting those sheet protectors into a three-ring binder makes photos accessible to children while safeguarding the photos. Similarly, using commercial photo albums that have plastic envelopes in which to insert photos allows children to handle photos without man-handling them.

LOOKING BACK/LOOKING AHEAD

This chapter has provided information about the technology tools related to implementing digital photography in early childhood classrooms. It has also alerted the reader to consumable materials to have on hand. The next, very brief chapter provides the user with a form to ensure that permission has been obtained to photograph the children in the classroom. It also alerts you to some concerns to address regarding policies for your center or school.

Two for the Show   **3**

Permission to Photograph Children

PHOTO RELEASE FORM

Permission is required to take photos of children. It is good practice to obtain a photo release from parents at the beginning of each school year. This release can become part of your annual paperwork. A sample release form is included on the CD with this book. Parents need to be assured that the photos of their children will be used for professional reasons only. Parents have the right to deny permission or to limit photo use to classroom use only.

Some families or members of some cultural groups may not give permission to have photos taken of their children because of a variety of reasons. If children are being excluded because parents won't sign a release, make sure to include those children in the products that are produced by having the children draw pictures of themselves. Take a photo of the children's drawings or use a scanner so that they can be digitized and dragged into applications just like a typical photo.

It is the ethical responsibility of the teacher to obtain informed consent when photographing. *Informed consent* means written permission to photograph and/or videotape a person or a person's work that is obtained from a parent or guardian of students under the age of 18, staff members, and volunteers (see Table 3.1 on page 45). In general, informed consent is obtained through photo release forms that address how photos may be used; for example, photos may be used in the classroom, for curriculum development, as a supplement to the educational program, for publication in school newsletters or brochures, for publicity in newspapers or other media, for research purposes, or on a Web site. Forms should allow parents to choose if photos may be taken or not, as well as how photos may be used. Parents should be assured that the child will not be identified by name on any photos used outside the classroom or on the Web site. It should be clear to parents that they relinquish any claims of ownership of the photo and that they will not be compensated for the photo. These forms need to be completed annually. (See Figure 3.1 for an example of a photo release form.)

To keep a record of permissions, Table 3.2 on page 45 is included on the CD for your convenience.

POLICIES RELATED TO PHOTOS

The teacher should consult with the program director or school administrator to discuss policies related to the use of photos outside the classroom. Can the teacher display photos on a hallway bulletin board if children are not identified by name? Can the teacher include photos in newsletters? Can the teacher post photos to the school's or center's Web page? Can the teacher include photos in a program brochure? The teacher also needs to know the policy regarding photos after the initial year. Will photos be stored or disposed of? Will photos become part of the children's portfolios that move with the children to the next classroom, program, or school?

LOOKING BACK/LOOKING AHEAD

This short but critical chapter has provided information about procuring informed consent to take and use photographs of children, as well as policies to consider when using photographs. The next chapter offers some tips related to photographing children.

Figure 3.1 Photo/Video Release Form

Photo/Video Release

Informed Consent form

For school year 20 __ – 20__

Please complete and return this form to the center or school as soon as possible. This information will be kept on file for reference throughout the school year.

Permission is hereby granted to YOUR SCHOOL NAME to take photographs/ videos of my child for professional purposes only. It is understood that photos may be taken by school or program personnel as well as by children enrolled in the school or program. I understand that I relinquish rights to the photos of my child and that no compensation will be paid to me for the photos. I understand that my child will not be identified by name in any of the photos used outside the classroom.

I grant permission to take and publish photos of my child for the following purposes (please initial your choices):

____ In-school use: Classroom displays, curriculum materials, class slide shows, or other educational uses

____ Out-of-school use: Classroom newsletters, school or center newsletters, and brochures

____ Community use: Newspaper articles or advertisements, publicity materials

____ Web site

____ Other: (EXAMPLE: photos for student teacher)

Permission to take photos is granted to the following (please initial your choices):

____ Classroom teacher(s) and children in the class

____ School or program personnel

____ Other parents or relatives of children at school or program events

____ Personnel from collaborating agencies (such as university supervisors, college students, etc.)

____ Media personnel (TV, newspaper, etc.)

____ Other (specify) _____

____ Permission is denied to take or use photos of my child for any reason.

Child's name _____

Parent's name (print) _____

Parent's signature _____

Date _____

NOTE: If circumstances change during the school year, you may change your consent at any time by contacting the center director or school principal in writing.

Table 3.1   Useful Sites Regarding Informed Consent

Development Photography Ethics: www.photoshare.org/phototips/developethics.php

Indiana Unversity—Bloomington, School of Education, Office of Research and Development, Informed Consent Checklist: www.indiana.edu/~edrsch/checklist.html

Winnipeg School Division, Informed Consent—Division Publications, Public Events, Media: ww.wsd1.org/board/policies_pdf/policy_KBAA.pdf

Table 3.2   Permissions Records

Child's Name	Permission Granted for:				
	In-School	Out-of-School	Community	Web Site	Other (specify)

Three to Get Ready **4**

General Photography Tips

This chapter will offer some general tips regarding considerations, timing, and techniques that will aid the teacher in getting good photos of children.

PREPAREDNESS

Be ready to photograph. That means having the camera around your neck. Always use the camera strap so that you won't have to worry about dropping the camera and damaging it; you are also being a good role model for when children start to use cameras. Make sure that your batteries are charged, but be cautious about recharging batteries when they are not drained, because this can affect the life of the batteries. Be aware that batteries can be drained by nonuse also. Get in the habit of checking the batteries at the end of each school day so they are charged for the next day. It is also a good idea to have an extra set of batteries fully charged and accessible for use. Always make sure that the camera is turned on and that you have the dial set for photographing rather than reviewing. Opportunities to capture expressions or a certain stage in a process can be lost if the teacher is not prepared.

EYE-TO-EYE

As any good early childhood educator knows, a teacher must get down to a child's level. The same is true when photographing children. If you shoot from above, the photo of the child will look distorted, with the child's head appearing very large. If you shoot from below, the child will appear to be all legs. So try to shoot straight on, eye-to-eye.

BACKGROUND

Be aware of the background of some of your photos, particularly those that you want to use repeatedly as a file photo, like face shots and full-body shots. These types of photos are typically posed against a plain background, so go out into the hall and have an X mark the spot where a child should stand or have a chair ready for the child to sit on for those posed shots. Of course, those candid shots in the classroom will capture your clutter, so this might motivate you to do some tidying up.

FREQUENCY AND FAMILIARITY

Candid shots of children are easier if the children are used to being photographed regularly. If the camera is only present occasionally, you are likely to capture those Cheshire Cat grins instead of genuine expressions of engagement. Catching a child unaware of the camera can best be achieved through familiarity or by using a telephoto lens and being outside the action.

BRIGHT LIGHTS

In most instances in a well-lit early learning environment, it is not necessary to use the flash. If you try to shoot photos in front of a window, pictures can appear washed out. A general rule is to keep windows at your back or to draw blinds or curtains when planning to photograph. Similarly, if you are shooting pictures outside, keep your back to the sun. When shooting outside, it may be difficult to use the LCD screen. If the camera has a Finder/LCD button, choose the Finder option for outside shots on a sunny day. This means that to frame a shot, the photographer looks through the camera's viewfinder rather than looking at the LCD, similar to what was done previously on a typical 35 mm camera.

OBJECTIVES

Consider what you are trying to capture with the picture. Do you want to show the child relating to others? If so, then look for times when the child is more social, like during choice times/playtimes/outside times. Do you want to show the kinds of materials to which a child is attracted? Then be ready to photograph the child with table toys or building with blocks or enjoying a book in the library center. Do you want to document a field trip? Be sure always to add a camera to your list of supplies for a field trip, guest speaker, or other special event.

POINT OF VIEW

Avoid being in the rut of always positioning yourself in the same place when you take photos. Move around your subjects to get a different angle on the action. For example, if you want to document children's writing skills, you don't want to have eye-to-eye shots; instead, you may want to shoot a photo over the children's shoulders as they write so you can use the photo to demonstrate what the children write or draw and how they hold their pencils or markers.

MULTIPLE SHOTS

Because digital cameras typically don't restrict the photographer to a minimum number of photos, don't be afraid to take multiple shots of the same subject or event. Because most of us are not professional photographers, it is best to shoot many pictures so that out of the many, perhaps one will be suitable for use.

CAUTION: DON'T BECOME PAPARAZZI

It can become tempting to overuse a digital camera. No one likes to be stalked continuously by the paparazzi. Always be aware of your objectives and inform children in advance when you might be taking photos; discriminate when you really need some photos for documentation or for a project. Explain your purposes to the children whenever possible. Some children do not like to be photographed at all, so it is best to respect their wishes if at all possible.

LOOKING BACK/LOOKING AHEAD

This chapter alerted the teacher to a variety of considerations and preparations when photographing in the classroom. The next chapter offers tips about record keeping to ensure that all children are included and that appropriate photos are being added to the photo database. It also offers some organizational strategies to help teachers make the best use of their time during this process.

Four to Go 5

Record Keeping and Organization

___

To use the digital camera in a systematic way in the classroom, it is critical to organize yourself to make sure that you are obtaining photos of each child and that you are obtaining the kinds of photos that you want of each child. It is also important to have a system in place to organize the photos and other data for ease of use. A good habit to establish is to download photos into files shortly after they are taken. This chapter will present some ideas to get the teacher organized.

RECORD KEEPING

Teachers are well aware of checklists, so this is another time to put together checklists for yourself to ensure that you are getting the pictures you want. First make sure that you have photos of each child's face (see Table 5.1) and one full-body picture of each child (see Table 5.2 on page 51). Store these photos in a file, whether on your desktop, on a CD, or on a flash drive. These photos will be used in numerous ways that will be explained later in this book.

Checklist of Photos of Faces

Table 5.1 Record Keeping: Photos of Children's Faces

Photos of Children's Faces School Year:	
Check if photo is in file	*Name of child*

Checklist of Photos of Bodies

Table 5.2   Record Keeping: Photos of Children's Bodies

Full-Body Photos of Children School Year:	
Check if photo is in file	*Name of child*

Checklists of Developmental or Academic Milestones

If you have decided to include photos of children in portfolios to demonstrate their knowledge, skills, and dispositions in developmental or curricular areas, then another checklist is needed for each child. Table 5.3 is an example of a preschool checklist; activities to photograph would need to be tailored to the child's age and developmental level.

Checklist for Special Events

If you want to produce a record of a field trip, holiday celebration, or another special event or if you are putting together a general slide show for an open house or parent conferences, be sure to have a checklist with you as you take photos so that you can make sure that each child is represented in some way at each event (see Table 5.4 on page 54).

ORGANIZATION

The photos become digital data, and data need to be organized. As mentioned previously, it is important to download the photos shortly after they are taken. Photos may be downloaded into photo management programs such as iPhoto on a Macintosh system or into files. Files can be established on the computer desktop; they can then be transferred to a storage unit such as a CD or flash drive.

To create a file within iPhoto on a Macintosh computer, first open the iPhoto program. Place the cursor on the File command on the toolbar. Scroll down to New Album and release the cursor. A window will appear that allows you to type in a name for this album. This file will appear in the index of files. Drag appropriate photos into this file. If you want to drag a whole series of photos into this file, click on the first photo. Next depress and hold the shift key. Move the cursor to the last photo in the series; click on the photo. Release the shift key; all the photos will be highlighted. Then place the cursor anywhere within the highlighted photos. Drag the cursor to the album. All the photos will be copied to that album. When you want to access photos in the album, click on the album, and only those photos will appear within the iPhoto display.

To create a blank file folder on a Macintosh computer, first click the mouse anywhere on the desktop while in the Word program. Then place the cursor on the File command on the top toolbar. When the dropdown menu appears, scroll down to New Folder. Release the mouse, and a blank file folder entitled "untitled folder" will appear on the desktop. Click on the highlighted title: "untitled folder." Type in a name for the file. Now you are ready to drag appropriate digital images into that file folder. Figure 5.1 on page 55 illustrates this process.

Table 5.3   Record Keeping: Photos of Children's Development

Developmental Portfolio Photos			
Name _____		**Reporting Period** _____ to _____	
Large Motor:	*Check:*	*Language:*	*Check:*
Ball skills		Talking on phone	
Coordination/ balance		Speaking during Show and Share	
Skill in riding wheeled toys		Listening to a story	
Arm strength			
Loco-motor skills		*Emergent Reading:*	
Other:		Looking at a book	
		Alphabet activity	
Fine Motor:		Other:	
Scissor cutting			
Drawing		*Emergent Writing:*	
Writing/printing		Printing name or other words	
Stringing			
Shoe tying		*Emergent Math:*	
Other:		Arranging by size activity	
		Pattern activity	
Social Development:		Counting activity	
Friends		Graphing activity	
Working together		Shape puzzles	
Type of play		Size cylinders	
Self-help Skills:			
Washing hands		*Emergent Science:*	
Brushing teeth		Magnet play	
Dressing		Watering plants	
Feeding self		Animal care	
		Sink/float activity	

Table 5.4   Record Keeping: Special Events Photos

Special Event Photos	
Check if photo is taken	*Name of child*

Figure 5.1   Establishing Files

To clear the desktop of clutter as you create digital files, create a master file folder and label it "Digital Images"; then drag all the other newly labeled folders into the master file.

General File for All Children

Throughout the school year, there will be multiple uses for photos of children's faces or full-body pictures of children. A good first step is to start collecting such photos and placing them in a file on your computer or other electronic storage device. Be sure to label children's photos with their names and dates so that you can find them easily when you want to use them for a project. You might organize a folder of face photos of all members of your class in a file called "Class Faces." You might also have a second file of full-body pictures of children in another folder entitled "Class Bodies."

In addition to a file on the computer, the teacher may choose to create a paper file of pages of photos printed in black-and-white or in grayscale. A master print copy can be used to duplicate as needed on a copy machine.

Files for Individual Children

In addition to the class files, it is recommended to start a file folder for each child so that you can collect photos for an individual child's slide show for conferences or to use in an electronic portfolio. Be sure to label each photo with a title and date.

Other Files to Consider

Other files to consider establishing could contain pictures to demonstrate your daily schedule of activities or pictures conveying themes, holidays, special events, or field trips. Some teachers might prefer monthly or quarterly files to correspond with assessment periods.

PowerPoint Presentations

Start a PowerPoint presentation for each child or each theme. As photos become available, drag them into a PowerPoint format so that the presentation grows over time. Working files such as this are best kept on the computer desktop or on a flash drive; CD-Rs do not work as well for this, because once a CD-R is burned, you cannot add to its contents. However, a CD-RW will permit storage and revision over time.

An example of a cumulative file is one containing photos of holiday celebrations. Each time a holiday is celebrated in your classroom or in the community, photos of the celebration are placed in a PowerPoint format so that a cumulative file emerges over time. By the end of the year, a slide show or a book, with or without text, is ready to print off. However, PowerPoint photo presentations tend to consume a lot of the computer's memory, so save that memory by burning the file to a CD-RW so that changes can be made as the presentation evolves. Alternatively, if you use a CD-R for storage, when you want to add to the presentation, you can open it, make changes that can be saved to the desktop, and then burn another CD-R with revisions before deleting the file from the desktop.

Clip Art

Clip art is a digitized graphic that is often imported into a product to enhance its ability to communicate. For example, if a teacher creates a book like *Timmy Had a Little Turtle,* an image of a turtle as well as a photo of Timmy would be included. However, teachers need to be aware of copyright laws when using such images. Fair use permits teachers to use copyrighted materials for educational purposes. According to the fair use chart provided at http://home.earthlink.net/~cnew/research.htm, teachers are directed to use "no more than 5 images of an artist/photographer in one program or printing and not more than 10% or 15% from published collective work, whichever is less."

Clip art is often available on the computer as part of the software associated with Microsoft programs. Additionally, clip art software can be purchased, or one can visit sites such as www.princetonol.com/groups/iad/links/clipart.html for images that are in the public domain. Copyright-free clip art is available for purchase at various sites such as www.clipart.com or http://classroomclipart.com/CRCLcopyright.htm.

If clip art is integrated into your products, it is advisable to establish your own file of clip art that is labeled and placed in folders related to themes. Having a file allows you to locate regularly used clip art images conveniently without having to go back on-line.

LOOKING BACK/LOOKING AHEAD

This chapter has provided checklists and ideas to get the teacher organized for collecting and managing photos for use in the classroom. The next chapter gives some pointers for using PowerPoint, the graphics presentation program that is utilized in many of the applications described in this book.

Getting to the Point **6**

. . . *PowerPoint, That Is*

POWERPOINT: A PRESENTATION SOFTWARE PROGRAM

This chapter will focus on one particular graphics presentation program, PowerPoint, mentioned in Chapter 2. PowerPoint is readily available to both Macintosh and PC users as part of the Microsoft Office Suite software package. Programs such as PowerPoint are updated from time to time, so the reader may need to adapt to those changes when they occur. Since many of the applications for digital photography that are presented in this book utilize the PowerPoint software program, it is necessary to explain briefly some basic manipulations within that program. It is also the program used for the templates that are provided on the accompanying CD. It is hoped that this chapter will encourage readers to gain skills with this program so that they can be creative and develop their own templates for future use.

A number of resource books are available that explain the PowerPoint program well and serve as tutorials. Some of these are listed in Table 6.1.

Getting Started With PowerPoint

It is necessary to have the PowerPoint program installed on your computer to use the CD that is included with this book. Microsoft Office is typically found in the "Microsoft Office" folder within the "Applications" folder on the hard drive. Once the PowerPoint program is loaded, if you have a Macintosh computer, it is handy to have it visible in your "dock," the toolbar that displays the icons for various programs. Drag the PowerPoint folder, the stylized orange *P,* to the dock. (See Figure 6.1)

When using the CD, it is not necessary to open the PowerPoint program. When you click on the icon for one of the templates, the PowerPoint

Table 6.1   Resource Books Related to PowerPoint

Finkelstein, Ellen. (2007). *How to do everything with Microsoft Office PowerPoint 2007.* New York: McGraw-Hill.

Lowe, Doug. (2007). *Microsoft Office PowerPoint 2007 for dummies.* Hoboken, NJ: Wiley Publishing.

Matthews, Carole. (2004). *Microsoft Office Powerpoint 2003: Quick steps.* New York: McGraw-Hill/Osborne.

Muir, Nancy. (2006). *Teach yourself visually: The fast and easy way to learn Microsoft PowerPoint 2003.* Hoboken, NJ: Wiley Publishing.

Negrino, Tom. (2007). *Creating a presentation in Microsoft Office PowerPoint 2007 for Windows.* Berkeley, CA: Peachpit Press.

Online Training Solutions, Inc. (2004). *Step by Step Microsoft PowerPoint 2003* (with CD). Redmond, WA: Microsoft Press.

Perspection, Inc., & Pinard, K. (1999). *Step by Step Microsoft PowerPoint 2000* (with CD). Redmond, WA: Microsoft Press.

Wempen, Faithe. (2007). *Microsoft PowerPoint 2007 bible.* Indianapolis, IN: Wiley.

Figure 6.1   The PowerPoint Icon in the Dock

program will automatically open. If you want to create your own product, open the program by double clicking on the icon.

When opening the PowerPoint program for your own use, a pop-up screen appears that offers the user choices for page settings (see Figure 6.2). Many of the applications for using PowerPoint with digital images in early childhood education employ the Title Page choice and the choices for inserting photos.

To choose a page selection, click on it until it becomes highlighted. Then click on the OK button in the bottom right corner. The selected page will pop up on the screen.

Figure 6.2 Page Selection Choices in PowerPoint

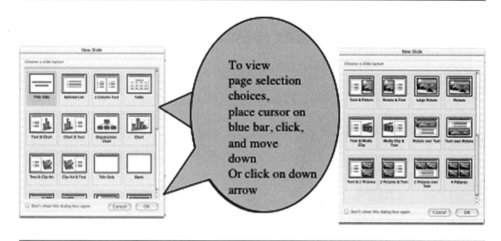

To add additional pages, place the cursor on the top toolbar, click on Insert, scroll down to New Slide, and release (see Figure 6.3). The page options will reappear, and the process is repeated as needed.

Figure 6.3 Insert New Slide

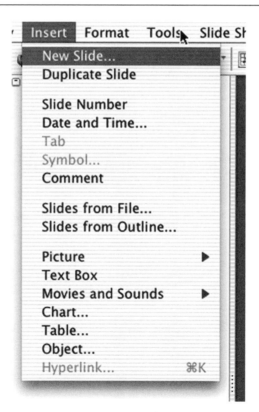

PowerPoint Viewing Selection Buttons

There are some icons on the bottom left of the PowerPoint page. These buttons offer viewing options (see Figure 6.4).

Figure 6.4 PowerPoint Viewing Selection Buttons

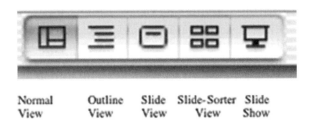

Typically, use the normal view or slide view when working within PowerPoint. When presenting a slide show, click on the slide show button.

Duplicating Pages Within PowerPoint

As projects are developed, sometimes text repeats from page to page. Rather than retyping the text on every page, it is faster to duplicate pages. (Please see the "Alphabet Book" template described in Chapter 9.) To duplicate pages, open the PowerPoint presentation to the slide that is to be duplicated. Then place the cursor on the top toolbar and click on Insert. When a dropdown menu appears, click on Duplicate Slide (see Figure 6.5). The duplicate page appears on the next slide.

Deleting Pages From PowerPoint

Using all the pages provided on the templates included on the CD may not meet your needs. In this situation, pages can be deleted. There are at least two ways to delete pages. One way is to place the cursor on the bottom PowerPoint toolbar so that you open the Normal View. In the Normal View, a slide is visible on the screen to the right, and a list of slides and their contents is visible on the left. Click on the minislide icon next to the number of the slide that you want to delete until it is highlighted, release the cursor, and click the delete button on the computer (see Figure 6.6). The slide is deleted.

Another way to delete a slide is to click on the Slide Sorter View on the bottom PowerPoint toolbar. Click on the slide that is to be deleted until it is highlighted and press delete on the computer keyboard (see Figure 6.7).

Inserting Text

There are at least two ways to insert text. One is to use the standard text boxes that are supplied within the program. The other is to insert a text box.

Figure 6.5   Duplicating Slides

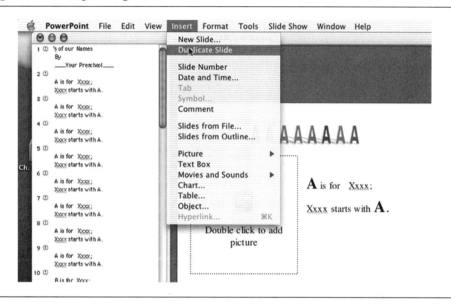

Figure 6.6   Deleting Slides in Normal View

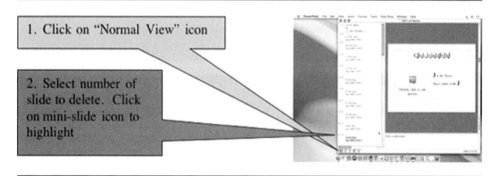

Figure 6.7   Deleting Slides in Slide Sorter View

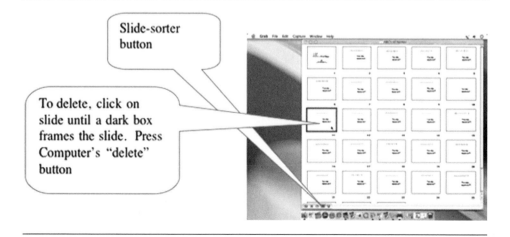

To insert follow the directions on the PowerPoint screen. For example, to add a title, place the cursor within the Click to Add Title box and start typing (see Figure 6.8). Wherever there is a box with a Click direction, you can insert text.

Figure 6.8   Inserting Text in Standard Text Boxes

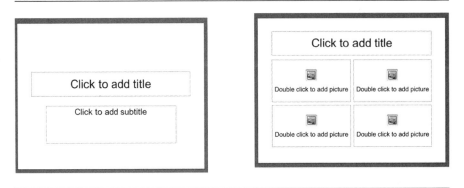

There are at least two ways to insert a text box to add more text in a different space on the page. One way is to place the cursor on the Insert function on the top toolbar, click, scroll down to Text Box, and release (see Figure 6.9).

Figure 6.9   Inserting a Text Box

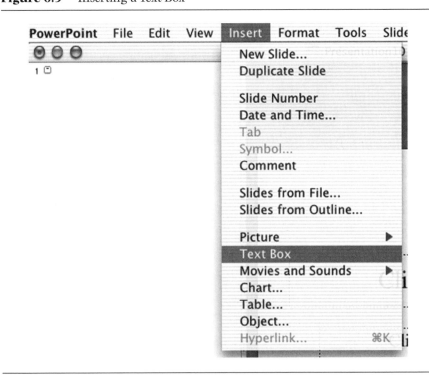

A letter *A* will appear where the cursor used to be. Move the *A* to the desired location on the page, release, and type in the text .

Another way is to use the Drawing Tool by placing the cursor on the View command in the top toolbar. Click and scroll down to Toolbars. Another pop-up menu will appear. Drag the cursor over and down and click on Drawing. The Drawing Toolbar will appear on the computer screen (see Figure 6.10).

Figure 6.10   The Drawing Toolbar

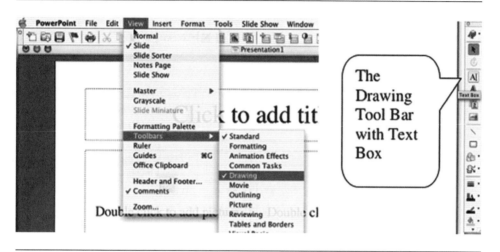

The Drawing options will appear. As shown in Figure 6.11, click on the text box symbol and release. An *A* will appear. Drag the *A* to the desired location for the text box. Click again, and a text box will appear. Type in the desired text.

It should be noted that when a PowerPoint presentation is printed out or viewed as a Slide Presentation, text box or photo frames do not appear; only images or text that is inserted is available for view.

Modifying Text Size or Font

Because PowerPoint screens are designed for presentation purposes, the font sizes are quite large. When using PowerPoint to produce printed materials, the font size can be reduced. To change the text size or font style in PowerPoint, place the cursor on the PowerPoint toolbar. Click on Format and scroll down to Font; a pop-up screen will appear (see Figure 6.12).

Select a font style by clicking on the down arrow or scrolling down the blue bar within the Font box. Click on the desired font style or type in the name of the font in the upper font box. Similarly, scroll down the blue bar or click with the up or down arrows in the size box to select a font size. Another way to choose a font size is to type the font size numeral in the top size box. Select any of the other features that you need on this page.

Figure 6.11   Inserting Text With the Drawing Toolbar Text Box

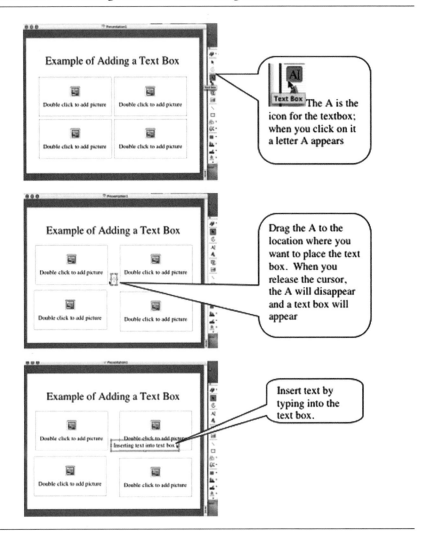

Figure 6.12   Changing the Font or Font Size

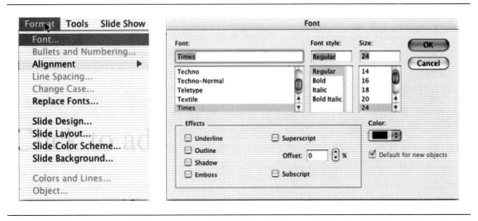

Resizing and Relocating Text Boxes or Photos

If you want to increase or decrease the sizes of the provided boxes or if you want to enlarge or downsize a photo once it is in PowerPoint, simply click on the box or image. As shown in Figure 6.13, small boxes, called "handles," will appear around the perimeter of the object. Click on a corner box (*not* a side box for photos, because manipulating the sides distorts images); another box with arrows will appear. Click and drag; move the handle outward to increase the photo's size and inward to decrease the size. When the image is the right size, release the handle.

If you want to reconfigure the standard PowerPoint page, you can move the boxes around by clicking on the object that is to be moved. When you place the cursor on the edge of a text box or on the face of a photo,

Figure 6.13   Resizing

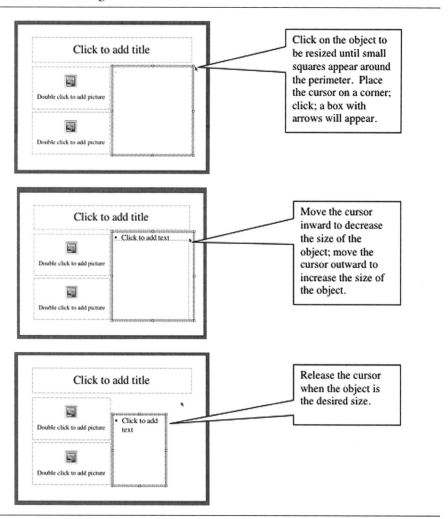

a hand will appear. When you click, the hand will grab the object. While clicking, drag the object to the desired location.

Importing a Photo Into Microsoft PowerPoint

Open the photo file on the computer. Open the PowerPoint page in which the photo will be inserted. Click on the photo that is to be moved; it becomes highlighted. Then, as shown in Figure 6.14, hold down the cursor and drag the photo to the PowerPoint photo box.

Figure 6.14   Dragging a Photo Into PowerPoint

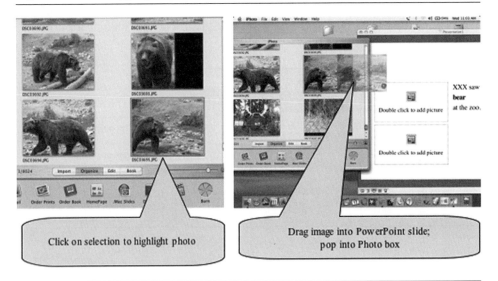

At first, photos may appear larger than the photo box; photos may even fill the entire screen (see Figure 6.15).

Figure 6.15   Large Imported Photo

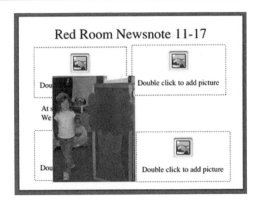

As shown in Figure 6.16, after clicking on the photo, boxes (handles) will appear around the perimeter of the photo. Click on the photo again, and the grasping hand will appear. Before releasing the mouse click, drag the photo to the center of the photo box; release the cursor. The photo will jump into the box and be instantly resized to fit the box.

Figure 6.16   Popping Photos Into PowerPoint

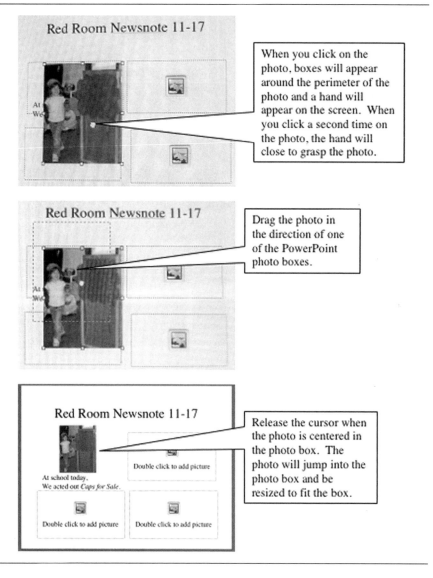

Rotating a Photo

Sometimes a photo is at an undesirable orientation. Drag the photo into the photo box as you did before. Once it is in place, click on the photo until boxes appear around the perimeter.

Move the cursor to the Drawing Toolbar. (If this toolbar does not automatically appear, you can find it by moving the cursor to the PowerPoint functions toolbar, clicking on View, scrolling down to Toolbars, and scrolling over to Drawing.) Click on the blue spiral shape for Free Rotate (see Figure 6.17). Green dots will appear in the corners of the photo. Move the cursor to one of the green corners. Click on and rotate the photo to the desired orientation (see Figure 6.18).

Figure 6.17 The "Free Rotate" Button

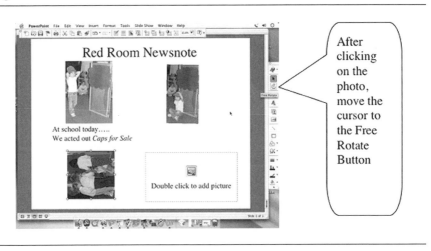

Figure 6.18 Rotating a Photo

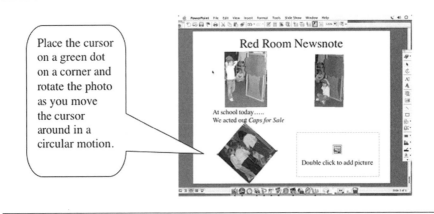

Return the cursor to the Free Rotate button. Click on it. Squares again appear around the perimeter of photos.

Copying Photos

Sometimes when creating in PowerPoint, the same image may appear on multiple pages. The photo can be repeatedly dragged into each page, or it can be copied from one page to the next, as shown in Figure 6.19. To copy a photo, select it by clicking on the photo until boxes (handles) appear around its perimeter. Move the cursor to the top toolbar. Click on Edit and scroll down the menu to Copy; release the cursor.

Figure 6.19   Copying a Photo From One Page to the Next Within PowerPoint

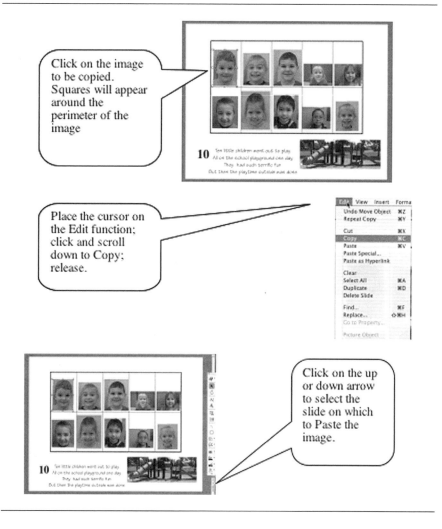

Click on the up or down arrow to move to another page where the copied photo is to be inserted. Place the cursor in the box in which you wish to insert the photo; click and release. Move the cursor to the Edit function on the top toolbar, scroll down to Paste, and release (see Figure 6.20).

Figure 6.20 Pasting Photos

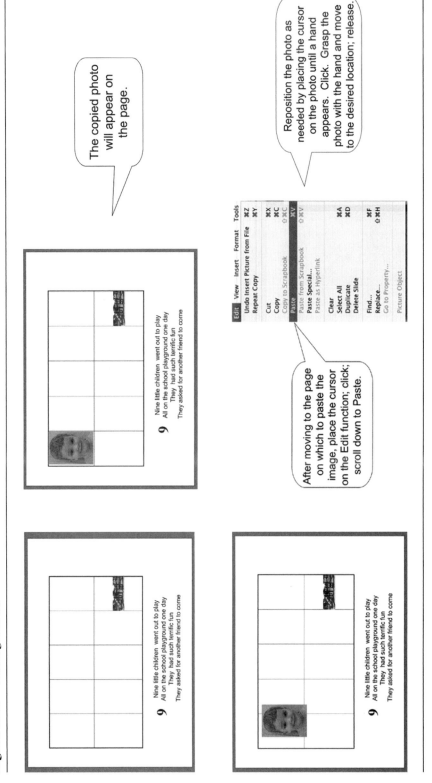

The photo pops onto the page. Place the cursor on the photo until the hand appears. Click to grasp the photo; drag the photo into the desired space. Save often within the PowerPoint program.

Inserting Clip Art

Insert clip art from the computer. Some clip art is typically provided with the computer. Other clip art programs are available for purchase.

To insert clip art from the computer, move the cursor to the toolbar at the top of the computer. Click on the Insert function, scroll down to Picture until it is highlighted, and move the cursor to the pop-up menu and highlight Clip Art (see Figure 6.21).

Figure 6.21   Inserting Clip Art

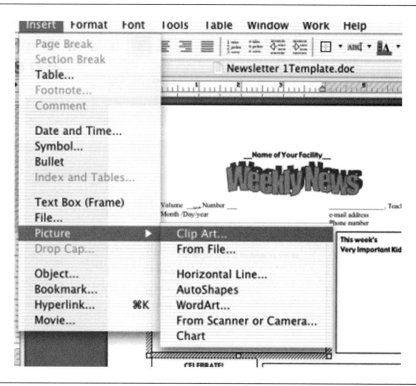

When you release the cursor, the Clip Art Gallery will appear. Type in the topic being sought in the Search box. An array of available clip art will appear to choose from. Either highlight and drag clip art into the newsletter or highlight and use the Insert function button at the bottom of the clip art program.

If the clip art needs to be resized, click on the clip art until boxes appear around the perimeter. Put the cursor on a corner handle (*not* side) box and move it in toward the center of the clip art to reduce the image's size or out from the corner to increase its size.

If the computer does not have clip art available or the available clip art does not meet your needs, clip art is available for purchase as a software program or online. Some sources were mentioned in Chapter 2. A search for clip art will locate other sources. Some sources are free, while some charge fees. Typically, copyright laws permit educators to use products for educational purposes in classroom settings. You may not sell a product with clip art that you have not purchased.

Saving Your Work

When working in PowerPoint, it is important to save your work often—don't wait until you have a finished product, because sometimes software programs quit unexpectedly. In fact, it is a good idea to save after completing each page. To save your PowerPoint product, place the cursor on the File function on the PowerPoint toolbar. Click and scroll down to the Save function; release the cursor (see Figure 6.22).

Figure 6.22   The Save Function

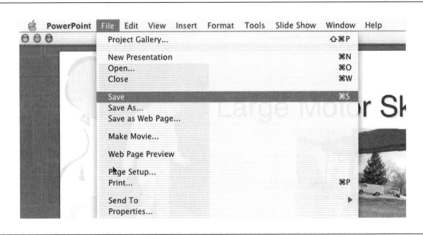

If this is the first time that you are saving a particular document, a pop-up page will appear. The PowerPoint program will automatically name the document Presentation1.ppt. To identify your document better, type a more appropriate title in this box. Before you click on the blue Save button, note where the file is being saved. You can save to your desktop or to another designated folder. Once you have named your file and saved it to a specific location, click the Save button (see Figure 6.23).

Figure 6.23   Saving a File With Name and Location

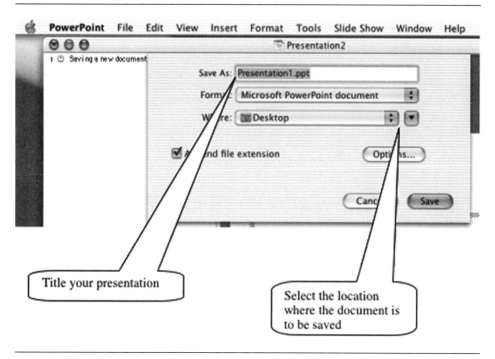

Title your presentation

Select the location where the document is to be saved

Notice that instead of Presentation1 appearing at the top of your working document, the new title appears. Continue to save the document by repeating the process of using the File menu on the PowerPoint toolbar, scrolling down and releasing the cursor on Save. As you continue to save after completing each page, the pop-up window will no longer appear. You may notice a flash as a blue bar moves across the bottom of the screen during the saving process.

If you are using one of the templates provided on the CD, you will need to use the Save As command, since you cannot save the template document on the CD. Proceed as before, accessing the Save As command by moving the cursor to the File command on the PowerPoint toolbar, then scrolling down to Save As and release the cursor (see Figure 6.24).

A pop-up window will appear. Rename the presentation. For example, if you are working in the "We Like Colors" template, rename it "Brown Class Likes Colors" (see Figure 6.25).

Figure 6.24   The Save As Function

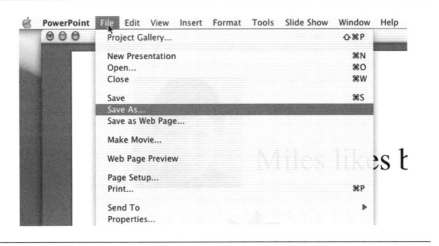

Figure 6.25   Renaming in the Save As Function

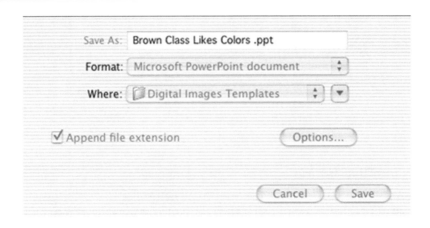

Print Options for PowerPoint

A variety of print options are available for the PowerPoint program. Some of these are related to size. The user can print one slide per page or choose to print two, four, or six slides per page. The more slides per page, the smaller the slides become. Documents may be printed in color, grayscale, or black-and-white.

To access the Print function, move the cursor to File on the PowerPoint toolbar. When you click, a menu of choices will appear in a drop box. Scroll down to the Print command (see Figure 6.26). When you release the cursor, the Print command window will appear.

Figure 6.26   The "Print" Function in PowerPoint

When you click on the blue arrows next to Copies and Pages, another drop down menu will appear (see Figure 6.27).

Figure 6.27   Selecting Pages to Print

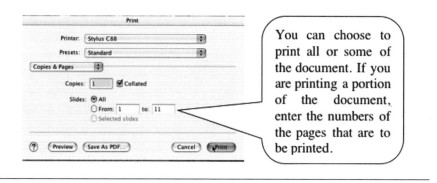

You can choose to print all or some of the document. If you are printing a portion of the document, enter the numbers of the pages that are to be printed.

As shown in Figure 6.28, scroll down to Microsoft PowerPoint. Release the cursor. In the Print What box, the word Slides will appear. If you want to print standard full-size pages in color, place the cursor in the blue Print button and release. If you want to print in black-and-white, place the cursor on the Output button and scroll down to Black and White. Then click on the blue Print button.

Figure 6.28   Microsoft PowerPoint Print Function

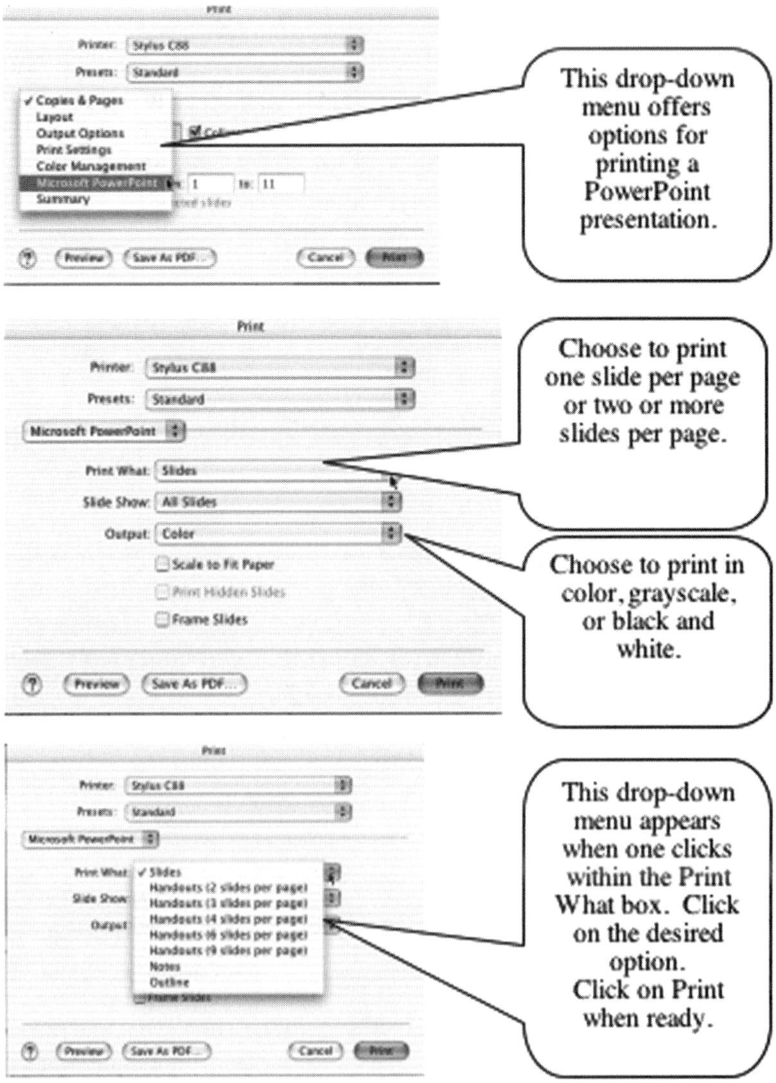

If you want to print in half-sheet size, place the cursor on the blue arrows by the Print What window and scroll down to command Handouts (2 slides per page).

Recording Voice Comments on Single Slides: A More Advanced Option

On occasion, teachers may want to record the children's voices as part of the PowerPoint slide presentation. Early childhood educators find it useful to have language samples of children as part of the assessment portfolio, and such language samples can be recorded into an electronic PowerPoint portfolio slide show. Additionally, sometimes a teacher puts together a slide show for the children, and recording their commentary adds to the presentation. For example, when the children go on a field trip, the teacher takes photos, prepares a slide show, and then invites the children to view the slide show and describe what they see on each page. While they are talking, the teacher records their voices. Later, the children and their parents may view the slide show and hear the children's narration.

To record their comments in PowerPoint, go to the Insert menu on the PowerPoint toolbar. Click and scroll down to Movies and Sounds and then scroll over and down to Record Sound (see Figure 6.29).

Figure 6.29   Finding the Record Sound Command

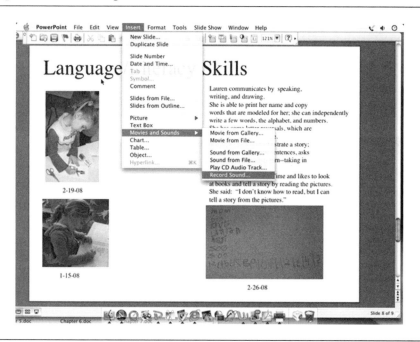

When you release the mouse, a pop-up screen will appear (see Figure 6.30).

At this time, you can name the sound by typing in a new title in the Name box; for example, "L's lang sample 4-5-08" (see Figure 6.31).

Click on the Record button when you are ready to record the voice or voices. Click on the Stop button to end the recording. Click on Save. The

Figure 6.30   The Record Pop-Up Screen

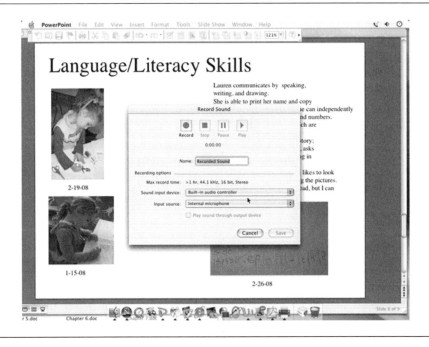

Figure 6.31   Naming the Sound

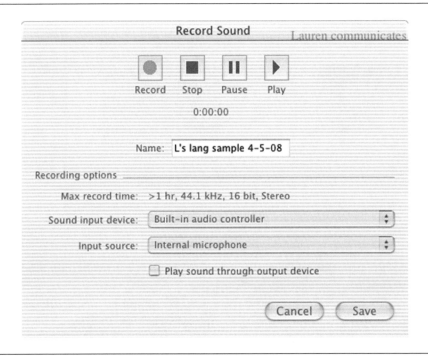

pop-up screen will disappear, and a sound icon will appear in the PowerPoint presentation (see Figure 6.32). When you click on the icon, you will hear the recorded message.

Figure 6.32   The Sound Icon

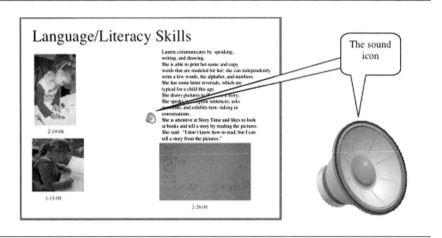

To adjust the volume of the sound, click on the volume control icon on the top toolbar (see Figure 6.33). Place the cursor on the circle. Move the cursor up to increase the volume; move the cursor down to decrease the volume.

Figure 6.33   The Volume Control

If you want to delete the recording, click on the sound icon and press the computer's delete key.

Other Advanced Options

When producing slide shows, teachers may want to include audio clips, as described above, or video clips. Hyperlinking is another advanced option to consider. Please consult one of the PowerPoint resource books listed earlier for instructions about how to incorporate these options.

LOOKING BACK/LOOKING AHEAD

This chapter offered guidelines for using both basic and some more advanced features of the PowerPoint program with digital photos. The next part consists of four chapters that provide tips for using digital photography in early childhood classrooms from preK through Grade 2. Examples of using digital photographs to assist with classroom management tasks will be presented in Chapter 7. Chapters 8, 9, and 10 will illustrate some examples of using digital photos to enhance curricula in the developmental domains.

Part III

Integrating Digital Images in PreK to Primary Classrooms

Photos as Aids to Classroom Management

7

The teacher in the early learning environment is a manager of people, time, and materials. This chapter will suggest a variety of ways that photos of children, materials, and the environment can assist the teacher in classroom management.

USING PHOTOS TO MANAGE PEOPLE

Using Photos for Taking Attendance

One administrative task that the teacher does daily is taking attendance. The teacher can designate this duty to the children upon their arrival with the help of photos.

One method is to situate a bulletin board near the door at the children's height. This bulletin board is divided into two sections: home and school/center. *Home* is depicted by a picture or icon of a house; *school* is depicted by a photo or icon of the school or center. Each child's photo is laminated and has either a Velcro strip or paperclip attached to the back. Corresponding Velcro strips on both sides of the board or on hooks are available to loop the paperclips onto. Prior to the children's arrival, all photos are attached to the board under the Home section. As children arrive, they move their photos to the School section. (See Figure 7.1.)

A second method is to print photos on magnetic paper or to laminate printed photos and attach a magnetic strip to the back of each photo; photos are placed on two large cookie sheets. Cookie sheets also have Home and School designators, or they might be color-coded by being

Figure 7.1   Taking Attendance

APPLICATIONS IN A PRIMARY CLASSROOM

- Class management: Create a photographic class list for substitute teachers so that they can easily identify the children when you are absent.
- Class management: Create photographic lists of group membership so that children can see who is in their group when the class is split into different working groups or learning stations.
- Class management: Create photo name badges to label children's folders or workbooks

spray-painted different colors. When the routine of checking in has been established, the teacher can take attendance at a glance.

Yet another way to take attendance is to make each photo into a necklace or attach it to a lanyard, such that children put their necklaces or lanyards on when they arrive.

Another attendance-taking method is to print photos of children on a chart. The children either place X's or print their names (an incidental writing experience!) next to their photos. (See Figure 7.2.)

Figure 7.2   Sign-in Attendance Chart

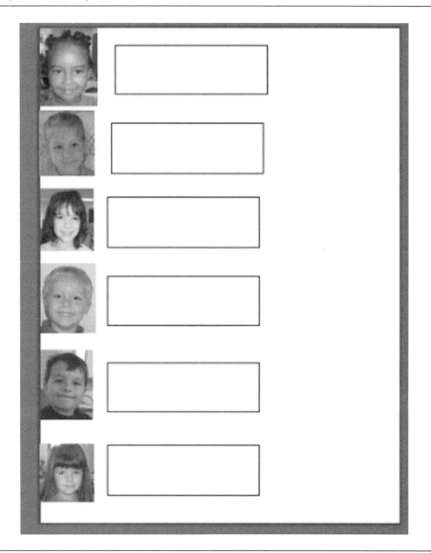

Using Photos to Assist With Plan/Do/Review

When the HighScope curriculum is used, teachers engage children in the "Plan, Do, Review" process. Photos can be used to help children make decisions about their plans and can also be used when children reflect on what they did. Photos of the choices should be prepared prior to the children's arrival. Then when it is time to "Plan," photos can be displayed, and children can choose activities using the photo cues. While children are in the "Do" phase, if possible, take photos of children engaged in their choices and quickly print them off for review time. At "Review," the children can use their language to describe what they see themselves doing in the photos. This is especially helpful for children with special needs or children who are learning English.

Using Photos to Assign "Jobs"

Teachers lead general meeting times or circle times daily in which routine activities take place. One of these routine activities is the assignment of jobs for the day. Teachers can produce a job chart that uses photos of children to designate jobs. Photos can also be produced that depict the jobs; for example, if care of the classroom pet is one of the jobs, a photo of the pet is included in the chart. When Velcro is used to attach the laminated photos to a job chart, the teacher can easily rotate children through the jobs by moving the photo within the chart. A less expensive alternative to using Velcro is using pins or hooks or making masking tape loops on the backs of the laminated photos.

Remembering Birthdays With the Help of Photos

Birthdays are special occasions. If birthdays are recognized and celebrated in the classroom, a classroom bulletin board of birthdays that places children's photos under designated months lets everyone in the room know when to anticipate a birthday celebration (see Figure 7.3). Another way to designate a birthday is to place a photo of the birthday child on the calendar for that month during circle time. Children can count up to the birthday in anticipation of the event.

Figure 7.3   A Birthday Chart

Using Photos to Limit Participation

For children to function in a self-directed early learning environment, one of the roles of the teacher is to structure the environment so that children can successfully navigate through the environment and through the day. Choice is a developmentally appropriate practice. To assist children in their choices, centers should be labeled, limits of participation for each center should be clearly communicated, and directions should be provided for some activities.

For children to be successful, it is necessary to impose participation limits to avoid overcrowding and negative behaviors or to ensure access to needed resources. There are many strategies for communicating limits: pegs on which to hang name tags, Velcro boards on which to attach name tags, tickets specific to each center, or learning center necklaces that children wear while participating in a center (Beaty, 1992). (See Chapter 1 for an example of a limit sign in an art center.) Photos can be used for any of these strategies. Photos of children's faces that are laminated and have Velcro on the back can be moved from center to center. Multiple photos of centers can be printed, and the number of photos for each center can indicate how many children can play there. For example, if there are four block center photos, four children can choose them to designate participation in the block center (see Figure 7.4).

Figure 7.4 Block Center Limit

Block Center

- Self-regulation: Create social stories. Carol Gray describes a social story as a description of "a situation, skill, or concept in terms of relevant social cues, perspectives, and format" (www.thegraycenter.org/store/). The goal of a social story is to improve a child's understanding of expected behaviors so that the child can attain more positive behaviors. To create a social story, first state the problem. Then use photos of the child acting out the appropriate behavior, tell why the behavior is appropriate, use another photo to show the consequences of appropriate behavior, and end with a confidence statement and another photo of the child. For examples of social stories, see http://rsaffran.tripod.com/social.html).

Using Photos to Communicate Expected Behavior

Photos can also communicate expected behaviors within a center or within a classroom. For example, in a game center, a picture of three or four children playing a game serves as a model to make children aware of how many can play a game. A photo of a child wearing a headset in a listening center illustrates that this is a quiet, one-person activity (see Figure 7.5). A photo showing "the right thing to do" can reinforce self-regulation in a primary classroom.

Figure 7.5   Photo Demonstrating What to Do in a Listening Center

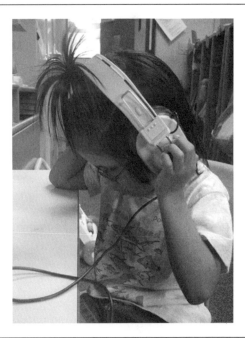

Using Photos to Provide Instruction

Center choice activities or learning centers permit children to play and learn independently. However, some activities require a process to allow children to complete the activity successfully. Process charts encourage emergent literacy while offering picture cues to children that serve as directions. Process charts show step-by-step directions to achieving a desired outcome (see Chapter 1). Process charts are particularly helpful for self-help, art, science, and cooking activities. Process charts are also useful as a social story for children who have difficulty with personal organization. For example, a process chart might be posted over a sink to demonstrate proper hand washing (see Figure 7.6).

Figure 7.6   Hand Washing Process Chart

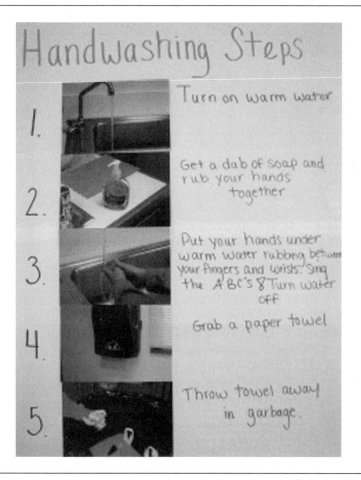

A process chart might be posted in an art center to demonstrate visually putting on a paint shirt, drawing on paper with a crayon, painting over the crayon with water colors, placing the artwork on the drying rack, washing hands, and removing the paint smock. Photo images are very good ways to communicate the process without relying solely on writing. Another example of a process chart is presented in Chapter 10 for a science activity.

USING PHOTOS TO MANAGE TIME

 A teacher manages time by establishing and posting a daily schedule that depicts the predictable sequence of events that typically occur during the day. Time is a difficult concept for young children, but using photos to show the sequence of activities communicates to the child what they have done within a day and what is yet to come. For the child in primary school who has difficulties with self-regulation and sequencing, a personal daily schedule can be presented in the form of a social story. A "Daily Schedule" template, shown in Figure 7.7, is included on the CD that accompanies this book.

Figure 7.7 "Daily Schedule" Template

 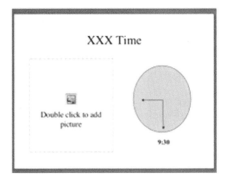

The user will delete the *XXX*'s, type in information appropriate to the program, and then drag in appropriate photos to depict what happens at that time of day (see Figure 7.8). Always remember to save frequently. To

Figure 7.8 "Sample of Schedule" Template Page

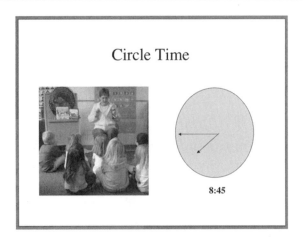

resize a photo, click on the image, placing the cursor on a corner handle, and move the cursor in or out as directed in Chapter 6. This template offers pages to record scheduled events within 15-minute increments from 7:00 AM to 6:45 PM, so users may select the most appropriate ones for their situations.

This schedule can be printed as a full page or as two slides or four slides per page, depending upon how much space is available for posting the schedule. See Chapter 6 for printing instructions specific to PowerPoint.

USING PHOTOS TO MANAGE SPACE

The typical early learning environment consists of many different learning centers. These centers might include alphabet, art, blocks, computer, dramatic play, games, library, manipulatives or table toys, math, music, science, sensory table, and writing. Beaty (1992) recommends labeling learning centers and suggests taking photos of each center to mount and place at the entrance to each. In addition to a photo of the center, the label for the center should identify it in words to promote literacy.

USING PHOTOS TO MANAGE MATERIALS

Photo Labeling of Materials on Shelves

Photos can be used to assist with clean-up activities, to help manage materials, and to help children learn responsibility. Dodge, Colker, and Heroman (2002), Gordon and Browne (2004), Jalongo and Isenberg (2004), and others recommend that storage shelves be labeled (see Figure 7.9). While it is always good to provide a literacy model of words, it is better to pair those words with pictures of the objects that belong in the space. Children can match objects to photos of objects and thus replace items in the proper storage space. In the past, teachers may have used catalog pictures or pictures from the box in which the object came. However, these deteriorate over time and may not be easily replaceable. When teachers take digital photos of toys and materials, they can create computer files so that these photos can be reprinted as necessary.

Figure 7.9   Labeling Storage Shelves

Using Photos to Inventory Materials

Creating a file of photos of materials, toys, and equipment can serve as a photo inventory of materials. As new toys, materials, or pieces of equipment are added to the classroom inventory, take photos of the objects and store them in an electronic file. See Chapter 5 for how to create files of photos. Separate files for different kinds of materials can be established. For example, photos of all the puzzles would be placed in a "Puzzles" file, while photos of all the children's books would be placed in a "Children's Books" file. Teachers could then use these files to search for appropriate materials related to particular themes. Or materials could be photographed and put in theme folders such that if the theme was "Community Helpers," teachers could open the electronic file and see photos of all materials related to this theme.

Digital images can greatly assist the teacher in classroom management tasks that involve children in successfully participating in learning.

> **APPLICATIONS IN A PRIMARY CLASSROOM**
>
> • Personal organization: Providing photos as a model of how to organize materials in desks, workspaces, or cubbies assists the child with maintaining order in personal spaces.

LOOKING BACK/LOOKING AHEAD

Many ideas were presented in this chapter to assist teachers with managing people, time, and materials in preK to primary-grade classrooms. The next chapter will focus on ideas for using digital photography to address emotional development goals when working with children.

Using Photos to Promote Self-Concept, Belongingness, and Security

8

Early childhood educators teach to the whole child. One of the domains that early childhood educators address is social/emotional development. Both preschool and primary-grade teachers focus on establishing a sense of community in their classrooms in which each member of the class is a valued participant. Elements of social/emotional development include the development of self-concept and self-esteem, as well as children's feelings of belongingness and security in the early learning environment. Photos of children can be used to address these areas.

USING PHOTOS TO PROMOTE SELF-CONCEPT

Self-concept and self-esteem are developed through the words and images that children hear and see about themselves. Perhaps one of the earliest foundations of self-concept is laid with the first hospital photograph of the newborn infant. As the infant grows into a child, photos are taken to document physical growth over time, milestones like annual birthday celebrations, and important relationships with family and friends. Photos record visual images of accomplishments: the first tooth, the first steps, dance performances, and athletic achievements to name a few. As family members review the photos with the child, the child hears "Look at you!"

or "Look what you did!" The photos and verbal messages contribute to the child's sense of self as well as the child's sense of self-worth or self-esteem.

Being the subject of a photograph is a self-esteem booster. When young children are photographed, they have a sense of being important. It is not uncommon to have young children willingly participate in photographs; in fact, they often beg: "Take a picture of me, teacher." Digital cameras with LCD screens allow children to see their images almost instantly. The children's smiles, the children's language, and the children's engagement with the photos all indicate that their images are important to them. (See Figure 8.1.)

Figure 8.1   Child Looking at Photo of Self

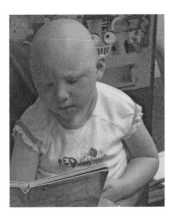

In an early study by Sponseller, Chisolm, Johnson, Plum, and Stenger (1979), photographs of young children with special needs were taken weekly to illustrate their interactions with materials, with peers, and with teachers. It was noted that there were significant increases in a self-concept measure after children experienced this photographic feedback for five weeks. In fact, six weeks after the study was completed, children were still looking at their photos and showing them to visitors.

A game that is used to identify emotions is a memory/matching game in which photos of children's faces expressing an array of emotions are duplicated; children then match the photos as they identify the emotion expressed (see Figure 8.2). Since young children on the autism spectrum often have difficulty discerning emotions, games like this can assist them in developing an awareness of facial expressions so that they can begin to read faces.

Figure 8.2 Matching Photos That Show Emotional Expressions

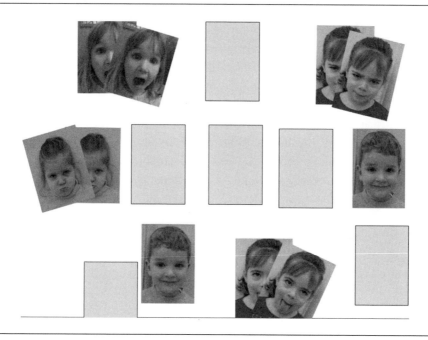

Yet another method that teachers use to help children identify emotions is the use of children's books (see Figure 8.3). Taking digital photos of children from a class and creating a digital book in PowerPoint is a way to create a bibliotherapy tool that is has specific meaning for a particular class. The "Feelings Book" template on the CD provides a format for such a book.

Figure 8.3 A Feelings Book Using Children's Photos

Indicators of self-concept development are children's awareness and expression of self in terms of characteristics, specific abilities, and preferences (Head Start Child Outcomes Framework Domain 6: Social & Emotional Development, www.headstartinfo.org/leaders_guideeng/domain6.htm). Photos of children help children to identify who they are in relation to others. They use the photos to compare and contrast themselves with others, noting similarities and differences of hair color, eye color, or other characteristics. In our multicultural, multiracial society, it is a recommended practice to use children's photos to teach about diversity and self-acceptance. One way to address diversity incidentally is to provide bulletin board displays of photos of children of each class.

Some activities that can help children differentiate self from others through the use of photos include a matching game, a categorizing game, or a graphing activity. To implement a memory game, print two photos of each child's face and laminate them. Children find pairs that match (see Figure 8.4). One can use these same photos as a categorizing activity. This time, only one photo of each child is presented, and children sort the photos by various attributes; for example, children could be directed to find photos of two children who wear glasses, find pictures of two children with blond hair, etc. A teacher-directed math activity could involve creating a graph such that children place their photos in the correct column related to some physical characteristic, like eye color; children then make judgments about the concepts of more, less, or the same related to those characteristics.

Figure 8.4   Matching Photos

Another way to use photos to assist children in developing a self-concept is to take photos of the children's fronts and backs; children then match the photos. Photos of children's faces and their profiles can be matched. Photos of children's faces can be cut in half and the children can match the two halves to form a whole face. An art activity related to self-concept involves printing the children's face photos on pieces of paper and then having the children draw in their bodies. (See Figure 8.5.)

Figure 8.5   Using Photos to Enhance Self-Concept

Drawing in a body

Matching Face to Profile   Matching Front to Back

When children are selected as the Very Important Kid or the Star of the Week and photos of the children and the children's favorite things or activities are publicly displayed in the classroom, the children develop a sense of acceptance and appreciation for who they are. An extension of this activity is to create a Star of the Week book; a "Star of the Week" template accompanies this book. It is an individual child's book that is published during or at the conclusion of the child being the Star of the Week.

An alternative to publishing an entire book is to print a Very Important Kid certificate to present to the child; a "Very Important Kid" template for such a certificate is included on the CD (Figure 8.6).

When using this template, the user should delete *XXX*'s and insert the child's name or other pertinent information. On the page that lists the child's favorite color, the user may elect to delete nonselected color choices or to have the child circle his/her favorite color after printing. The user should also plan ahead to gather appropriate photos and information to insert. Photos of the following may be part of this book: child's face, the child wearing a favorite color or painting with a favorite color, the child's favorite food, the child's favorite animal, the child's favorite toy, the child's favorite book, the child's best friend, the child engaged in a favorite activity,

APPLICATIONS IN A PRIMARY CLASSROOM

- Attach a photo of the child to artwork that is displayed.
- Attach a photo of the child to a child's autobiography.

Figure 8.6 "Very Important Kid" Template

a photo or drawing of the child's family, and a photo or drawing of the child's career aspirations. The child can draw some of these images (favorite food, favorite animal, favorite toy, favorite book, career aspiration), or images can be downloaded from clip art sources. Always remember to save frequently while in the process of producing the book.

USING PHOTOS TO PROMOTE BELONGINGNESS AND A SENSE OF COMMUNITY

When children enter an environment and see their images being a part of that environment, they have a sense of belongingness that contributes to their inclusion in a community of learners. (See Figure 1.1, Bulletin Board of Members of the Brown Class.) A bulletin board that is labeled "Our Day at School" can be a place to display photos of children engaged with materials and people. As new photos become available, photos can easily be added or subtracted from the display.

An extension of a day-at-school bulletin board is the creation of a book about the children's day at school. One of the templates included on the accompanying CD is entitled "Day at School" template. (See Figure 8.7.)

Figure 8.7   "Day at School" Template

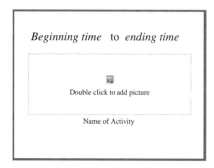

Photos of children engaged in activities at different times of the school day can be inserted into this template, and then the book can be printed (see Figure 8.8). (Insert photos as previously directed in Chapter 6. Type in information in place of *Beginning Time* and *Ending Time* and delete *Name of Activity* and type in a descriptor. Print as previously directed in Chapter 6.) Remember to save frequently while in the process of producing this book.

Figure 8.8   Data Entered in "Day at School" Template

8:00 A.M. to 8:30 A.M.

Quiet Activities

The pages can be inserted in plastic protector sleeves in a three-ring binder so that after the teacher shares the book with the children, it can be placed in the book corner for the children to look at and "read."

Another template that relates to the child's belongingness at school is the "I Go to School" template (see Figure 8.9). This is meant to be an individual child's book.

Figure 8.9　"I Go to School" Template

Photos of the child on the child's birthday, the school building, the child's teachers, the child interacting with friends, the child's favorite thing to do at school, and the child engaged in activities at school can all be dragged into this PowerPoint template. Remember to save frequently while in the process of producing this book. (See Chapter 6 for directions related to printing choices.)

Other templates featured on the CD that relate to belongingness are the "Our School Year" and "Favorite Activities" templates.

Private spaces for children within the classroom can also be labeled with their photos and their names. Photos can be used to label stationary spaces like lockers or cubbies. Photos can also be used to designate private portable spaces, such as place mats or carpet squares, by putting photos with children's names on these objects. Be sure to laminate photos for these uses.

USING PHOTOS TO BUILD SECURITY

Very young children may experience separation anxiety when parents drop them off for child care or early learning experiences. Teachers and caregivers can comfort children by having personal photo albums for the children with photos of their family members. Digital photos of parents can be taken as they pick up their children to remind children that Mom or Dad will be coming back; such photos will require another permission form to be signed. Another option is to solicit photos from families to place in an album for the child.

While in the early learning environment, children can also match photos of themselves to their families on an interactive bulletin board or as a tabletop activity.

Educators are required to be mandated reporters to ensure the safety and security of children. The digital camera is a useful tool when visible signs of suspected child abuse are present. In addition to documenting what is observed by recording the name of the child, the date, and a description of the physical signs, photographs can be taken of the bruises or burns and added to the file. Be sure to date the photos. An immediate phone call to the proper authorities is warranted, and, if requested, the digital photographs can be e-mailed to the proper agency.

LOOKING BACK/LOOKING AHEAD

This chapter presented ideas to assist teachers in fostering emotional development in children by using photos in a variety of ways. The use of photos to promote self-concept, belongingness, and security contributes to addressing children's needs in the social/emotional domain. The next chapter will explore another developmental domain, language and literacy.

Using Photos to Promote Language and Literacy 9

The early years are critically important times for language and literacy development. The National Association for the Education of Young Children and the International Reading Association issued a joint position statement in 1998 entitled *Learning to Read and Write: Developmentally Appropriate Practices for Young Children.* This document notes that literacy learning is an interactive process (www.naeyc.org/about/positions/psread2 .asp). Some recommended practices include reading aloud to children, exposing children to print, instructing about the alphabetic principle, and playing linguistic games and songs (www.naeyc.org/about/positions/psread1.asp).

Emergent literacy is inclusive of reading, writing, speaking, listening, viewing, and illustrating. The preprimary years are times of explosive vocabulary acquisition; according to Puckett and Black (2005), "young children learn and remember an average of 9 words a day from the onset of speech until age 6" (p. 394). The early learning environment fosters early language and literacy development for both English-speaking and English-learning young children. Children learn to take turns speaking and listening. Children learn language by interactions with adults and peers. Children first learn about books by caregivers reading to them and then learn to decode words and read for themselves. Children learn to draw and write when given opportunities and materials. Young children begin to make the connection between the spoken word and the printed word. Primary-grade children transfer their ideas on paper through writing and illustrating.

USING PHOTOS TO ENCOURAGE SPEAKING

To encourage speaking, wordless picture books are sometimes used with children so that they can interpret and describe what they see in the book's pictures. For example, Turkle's (1976) *Deep in the Forest* visually inspires children to talk about a twist on the Goldilocks story when a bear enters a cabin and emulates the antics of Goldilocks in the familiar story. Lehman's (2004) *The Red Book* takes the reader on a journey through the illustrations of a young child finding a red book with maps of other lands and follows the child as she travels. *Noah's Ark*, illustrated by Peter Spier (1977), is another wordless book that encourages the reader to talk about the illustrations as a story unfolds.

Similarly, wordless picture books can be created with the use of photos. A series of photos might be used to create a classroom's wordless picture book. For example, a classroom book might show children boarding the bus, arriving at the zoo, seeing various animals, and then boarding the bus to return to the center. Another form of a wordless picture book is a photo album. Such an album might contain a variety of pictures of children engaged in activities or playing with peers. It can be placed in the reading center where children can look at it and discuss it with friends.

Young children's language can be promoted by showing them photos and asking them to describe what is happening in the pictures. Because children are egocentric in the preschool years, they become engaged in photos of themselves. Throughout the school year, photos of children doing activities or participating in field trips can be taken. These photos can then be used as props during Show and Share Time, when a pictured child can describe what is happening in the photo. Photos might also be used to write a language experience story. In this way, children describe the picture while the teacher writes the child's exact words; thus, children begin to see a connection between the spoken word and the printed word.

USING PHOTOS TO BUILD VOCABULARY IN A BILINGUAL OR MULTILINGUAL CLASSROOM

TEACHER STATEMENT 1

I made *Friend, Friend, Who Do You See?* books for the children in my class and they LOVE them!! Especially my ELL children.

—Jennifer Slipka Head Start Teacher

SOURCE: Courtesy of Jennifer Slipka. Used with permission.

English-language learners, as well as children who are deaf, benefit from seeing pictures to illustrate what is being communicated orally. Photos provide a context for understanding. Photos may be used throughout the school day to convey a message. For example, during Circle Time, a photo of the topic being studied would convey that message to all participants. Likewise, a job chart would list jobs with both photos and written descriptions; when a child is selected to do a job, a card with the child's printed name and photo could be attached to that part of the job chart. A schedule can have photos that represent the sequence of activities for the day; when a teacher points to the photo on the daily schedule while saying the words to describe the activity, the child has a clearer understanding of what will occur next. When children see a process chart in a learning center, they can look at the photos while the teacher says the words to explain the directions for the activity. Toys or materials on shelves can also be labeled by taking photos of them. Photo labels with text in the appropriate languages can be placed on the shelves to communicate where to return materials. As materials are returned, teachers can use the bilingual labels as a crutch to reinforce the dual languages by orally labeling the objects in both languages.

When children are learning English or another language, simple photos of common objects can be taken. The photos can then be labeled with words in the child's native language as well as with words in English and/or other desired languages (see Figure 9.1). The photos can be printed as flash cards or as pages in a bilingual picture dictionary. These materials can be used at school as well as sent home to share with parents.

Figure 9.1   Labeling Photos in Multiple Languages

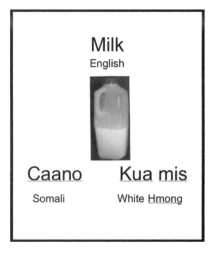

Special education teachers often use the Boardmaker program to produce visuals for young children with special language needs. "Boardmaker is a software program that uses clip art of picture communication symbols which are used in creating printed communication boards, device overlays, worksheets, and schedules" (http://groups.yahoo.com/group/boardmaker/). It is a product of Mayer Johnson (www.mayer-johnson.com). You can create similar results by using your own photos with the child as the subject; this makes the visuals even more appealing.

USING PHOTOS TO ENCOURAGE LISTENING

A teacher may use photos to tell a story and to increase children's vocabularies. For example, if the children are engaged in a farm unit, the teacher might show the children some pictures of farm animals and tell them some facts about the farm animals. For another example, a teacher might show a picture of a horse and then proceed to tell the children the type of horse it is and that male horses are called stallions, female horses are called mares, and baby horses are called foals. Or if the children are studying seasons, photographs of the same tree in the school playground during the different seasons could be taken and shown to the children. The children could listen as the teacher describes the tree in spring, summer, fall, and winter and point out the differences in the tree's appearance in the different seasons.

USING PHOTOS TO ENCOURAGE WRITING

Primary-aged children can use photos as writing prompts. Photos can be imported into PowerPoint such that there is one photo per page with space for writing next to it. At the writing center, children can be encouraged to write about what they see in the picture. School-age children may use a word wall or picture dictionary to assist them with spelling.

The writing of very young children may look like scribbling, but they can read their own writing and communicate orally about their writing. Older preschoolers may be able to print some letters, or they may be able to trace or copy words. The teacher might ask the children what they want to write about the picture. The teacher could then use

---

APPLICATIONS IN A PRIMARY CLASSROOM

- Reading and Writing: Adaptation of *Flat Stanley*: Many teachers extend Jeff Brown's (2003) book Flat Stanley by having children create a flat person as an art project. An autobiography is written about the flat person. The flat person, the autobiography, and a journal are mailed to someone who hosts the flat person and writes about its visit. Eventually, the flat person is mailed back to the child. Instead of producing a "*Flat Stanley*" figure, use full-body photos of the children in your class. Children can write an actual or fictional autobiography and then mail the photo, autobiography, and journal to someone. Recipients of the flat child might take photos of the flat child during their visit to return with the written account of the flat child's visit. For another technological idea related to *Flat Stanley*, visit www97.intel.com/en/ProjectDesign/UnitPlanIndex/FlatStanley/

a highlighter pen to write the words so that the child can trace the highlighted letters, thus writing about the picture. Word/picture cards can be used to scaffold the child's learning by providing models to copy. For example, for the picture in Figure 9.2, the words *snow* and *sled* could be provided as models for the child to copy.

Figure 9.2   Photos as Writing Prompts

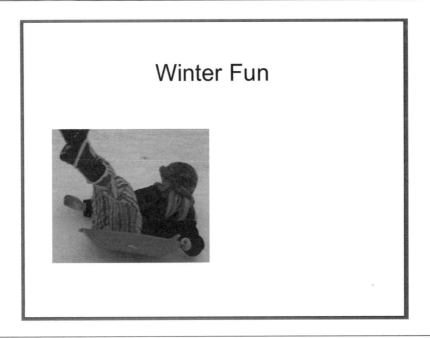

Another authentic way to encourage writing skills in young children is to have them write a thank-you note. Typically, thank-you notes are written to guest speakers, classroom volunteers, guest musicians, guest storytellers, or to a business or agency when a field trip is taken. When a photo of the guest or field trip site is part of the thank-you note, the children have a visual prompt to remind them about the event as they are writing. Children might write messages or merely sign their names. (See Figure 9.3.)

PROMOTING ILLUSTRATING THROUGH THE USE OF PHOTOS

Children can add to a photo with illustrations. For example, when firefighters visit the class as guest speakers, be sure to take photos of them. Then have the children draw pictures around the photos to illustrate some of the tools that the firefighters demonstrated. Perhaps some of the children will draw a fire truck, others will draw a fire hose, and still others

Figure 9.3   Photo as Part of Thank-You Note

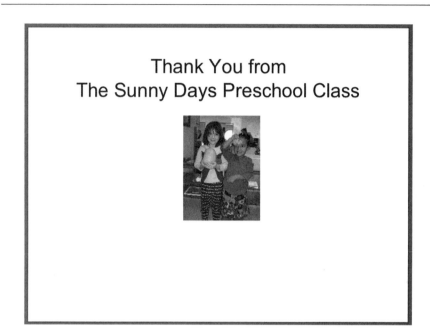

might draw the firefighter's mask. Figure 9.4 is an example of a photo that children have further illustrated to tell a pictorial story.

Figure 9.4   Using a Photo to Encourage Illustration

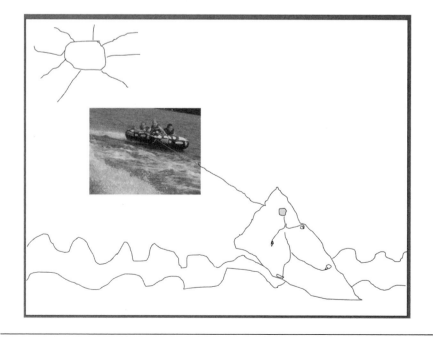

USING PHOTOS TO ENCOURAGE READING

TEACHER STATEMENT 2

Each week I visit day cares and read two stories having to do with developmental assets. Then I share a personalized book with them. I create these books by photographing the children and inserting their pictures and names into one of the templates. After printing them on cardstock, I put them in heavy duty plastic sleeves and then in a 3-ring binder. The binder has a see-through plastic cover that allows me to put a title page containing the child's picture and name (i.e., Becky's Book). The book then stays at the day care for everyone to look at and will eventually go home with the child. Each day care is also getting a book created with all of the children who attend that day care. I have had an incredible response from the children who have received their books already. One day care provider said she has read her son's book to him "about a hundred times" in the two weeks since he received it. The kids are very proud of their books and become very protective of them. Just today one of the 2-year-old girls took her book off into a corner to look at, and she sat on it when anyone else tried to get to it! (See Figure 9.5.)

—Becky Tish
AmeriCorps READS Initiative Member

Figure 9.5   Children Enjoying Personalized Books in a Day Care Home

Reading for young children is both a passive and an active process. Children passively learn to read by being read to. As children become actively engaged in the emergent reading process, they seek out picture books that use illustrations or photos to give context to the story. Using

picture books, children learn to read the pictures first, then they notice the print, and then they attempt to decode the print. The use of repetitive text is often recommended for young children who are just beginning the emergent reading process. The following sections offer some ideas about how to create books by inserting children's photos into the templates provided on the accompanying CD.

TEACHER STATEMENT 3

Dr. Good's book templates are a great way to get students excited and involved! The CD of templates has all of the work done for you with spaces left to add in any personalized information such as names or pictures.

—Katie Deutsch
College Student

SOURCE: Courtesy of Katie Deutsch. Used with permission.

Encouraging Emergent Readers

Young children come to kindergarten or first grade with the expectation that they will learn to read. Using the "We Can Read" template can assure children that they are already readers because they can decipher the symbols on neighborhood signs. When they see their pictures next to symbols that they can read, they are motivated to decipher other symbols.

Producing an Alphabet Book

Alphabet books are favorites among the preprimary or kindergarten set. As children are beginning to recognize letters and sounds, alphabet books are good tools for teaching the alphabetic principle. Children are especially interested in finding the letter of the alphabet with which their own names begin. With the use of digital photography, a personalized alphabet book can be created for each class. An "ABCs of Names" template is provided on the accompanying CD.

One page is provided for each letter of the alphabet. To create an alphabet book, open the title page (as pictured in Figure 9.6) and delete "Your school or center"; type in the name of your center. Advance to the next slide by placing the cursor on the down arrow and clicking (see Figure 9.7).

Advance to a page with the letter that is the beginning letter of a child's name in your class. Drag in a photo of the child from your photo file. Delete the X's and type in the child's name. Save often. Because one cannot save to the CD, use the "Save As" function and rename the book for

Figure 9.6   The "ABCs of Names" Template

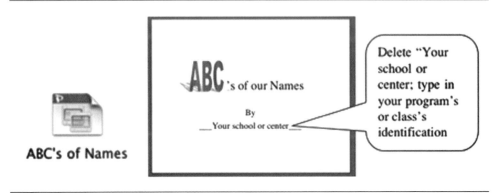

Figure 9.7   Advancing to the Next Slide Within the Templates

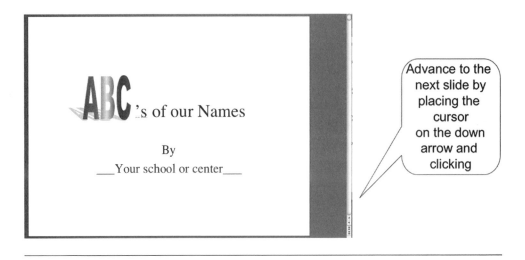

your class by typing in a name like "Our ABC Book." After a new file is created, such as "Our ABC Book," the "Save" function can be used as you complete the process. (See Figure 9.8.)

  If more than one child has a name that begins with a particular letter, duplicate that page. (Please see Chapter 6 for directions on copying a page.) Repeat this process as often as needed for as many letters as needed. It is likely that not all letters of the alphabet will be needed for the names of the children in the class. One alternative is to drag in some images from clip art to correlate with the remaining letters. Another alternative is to delete the unused letter pages. (Please see Chapter 6 for instructions on how to delete pages.)

Figure 9.8   Before and After Inserting Text and Photo Into an "ABCs of Names" Page

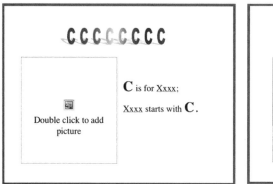

Save frequently as you add photos and children's names. Print the final copy as directed previously in Chapter 6.

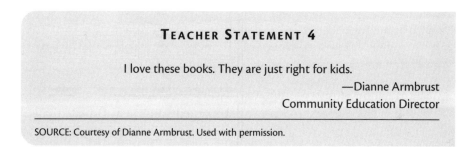

TEACHER STATEMENT 4

I love these books. They are just right for kids.
—Dianne Armbrust
Community Education Director

SOURCE: Courtesy of Dianne Armbrust. Used with permission.

Creating Concept Books

Young children are learning some basic concepts related to colors, shapes, and numbers during the preschool years. Several templates to reinforce these concepts while personalizing them with children's photos and names are included on the accompanying CD (see Figure 9.9).

Figure 9.9   Templates to Reinforce Concepts

Counting Fruits
Template.ppt

Playground Template.ppt

Ten Little Friends
Template.ppt

We Like Colors .ppt

We Like Shapes.ppt

When using the "We Like Colors" template (see Figure 9.10), drag in a photo of a child for each color page. There are pages for the following colors: red, yellow, orange, brown, green, blue, purple, black, white, and pink. If it is necessary to duplicate pages, do so as instructed in Chapter 6. Print as directed in Chapter 6. Always remember to save often while in the process of creating this book. Again, because a new file with photo inserts is being created, the first time the new book is saved, the Save As function should be used.

Figure 9.10   Pages From "We Like Colors" Template

The "We Like Shapes" template is similar (see Figure 9.11). Delete the *X*'s from the Title Page and type in the name of the class. On each page, delete the *X*'s and type in a child's name; then drag the child's photo onto that page. There are pages for the following shapes: circle, oval, crescent, equilateral triangle, isosceles triangle, square, rhombus, rectangle, parallelogram, diamond, trapezoid, pentagon, hexagon, octagon, heart, cylinder, and cube. To add or delete slides, follow the instructions in Chapter 6.

Figure 9.11   Pages From the "We Like Shapes" Template

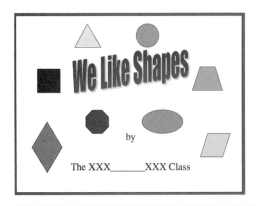 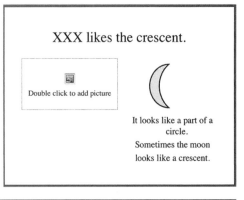

Always remember to save often while in the process of constructing the book. Because a new file with photo inserts is being created, the first time the new book is saved, the Save As function should be utilized. Print as directed in Chapter 6.

TEACHER STATEMENT 5

My seven-year-old daughter spent two hours looking at her personalized book featuring her. She shows it to everyone, slept with it the first night, and brought it to school for sharing. What an awesome idea!

—Becky Tish
Parent

SOURCE: Courtesy of Rebecca Tish. Used with permission.

The "Ten Little Friends" template (see Figure 9.12) results in a counting book, but the template for this book is limited to inserting photos of ten children. Duplicates of the book can be made for adding additional children's photos. This template only requires that photos be dragged into place. Because a new file with photo inserts is being created, the first time the new book is saved, the Save As function should be employed. After creating the new file, the Save function can be used. Print.

Figure 9.12 Pages From the "Ten Little Friends" Template

 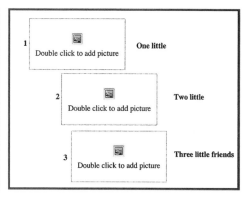

The "Playground" template (see Figure 9.13) is used to create another counting book. The template is limited to inserting the photos of ten children, so it may be necessary to print duplicate books for classes with more than ten children. Since photos of children are duplicated from page to page of this book, it is recommended that you begin by

Figure 9.13   Pages From the "Playground" Template

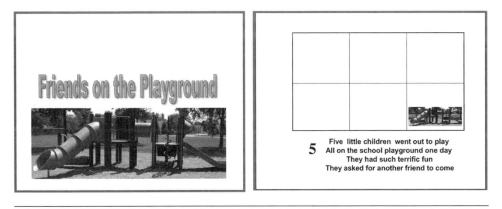

inserting photos into the last page first, then copying the photos, minus one per page, to each preceding page. (See Chapter 6 regarding copying photos to different pages.)

Inserting photos in this book requires a little more manipulation, since the PowerPoint photo boxes are not available. Drag the photo from the file into the PowerPoint page. If the photo needs to be reoriented, use the Free Rotate button as explained in Chapter 6 (see Figure 9.14).

Figure 9.14   Using the Free Rotate Button to Reposition a Photo

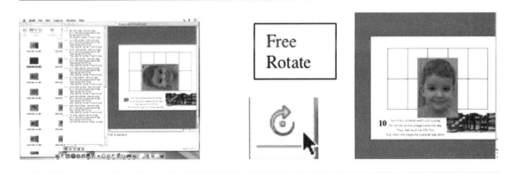

The photo is too large to fit into a box and will not pop into the box as it does with the PowerPoint Photo box, so the photo needs to be resized and then grabbed, moved, and centered into one of the boxes. (See Chapter 6 for instructions on how to resize objects.) Remember not to resize using a handle on the side of a photo, because doing so would distort the photo. Only use the corner handles when resizing a photo. Repeat this process until all the boxes are filled. (See Figure 9.15.)

Remember to save frequently. The first time this file is saved, use the Save As function to create a new file. Once a file is established, one can utilize the Save function.

Figure 9.15   Resizing and Repositioning a Photo into the "Playground" Template

This template requires that photos be copied from page to page; some photos are repeatedly copied on each page. (See Chapter 6 regarding directions for copying photos within the PowerPoint program.) Print.

"Counting Fruits" is another template that results in a counting book (see Figure 9.16). The template for this book requires similar electronic manipulations. This book is designed for a maximum of 17 children.

Figure 9.16   Pages From the "Counting Fruits" Template

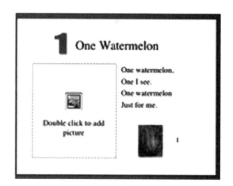

As with previous templates, the title page requires that the X's be deleted and the name of the center or school or class be inserted. The other pages require dragging the child's face photo into the PowerPoint photo box. Children's photos may need to be rotated as was explained in Chapter 6. (See Figure 9.17.)

Creating Books That Are Piggybacking Familiar Stories

Raines and Canady (1989) encouraged the expansion of children's favorite books with *Story S-T-R-E-T-C-H-E-R-S*. They suggested that activities

Figure 9.17   A Completed Page From the "Counting Fruits" Template

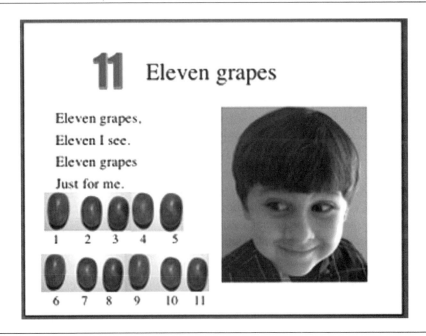

- Language Arts: Create your own books with photos to demonstrate synonyms and antonyms.
- Language Arts: Create a book that emphasizes the concepts of proper nouns and common nouns with photos.
- Phonics: Have children create their own books of sounds by taking photos of objects that begin with the same sound.
- Language Arts: Create a book of verbs by snapping photos of children acting out the action words.
- Language Arts: Create a book about idioms using photos of the children acting out the idioms (e.g., "being all tied up").

related to favorite books expand the story into other curricular areas to promote children's interest in reading. Jean Warren's (1983) *Piggyback Songs* put new lyrics to familiar tunes. Combining these two ideas, Story Stretchers ideas can be extended through a piggyback version by the use of digital photos to create books that personalize and extend the storylines of familiar children's books. When children find their pictures and names in a book that is similar to one already familiar to them, the children's motivation and interest in and enthusiasm about the reading process increase. The children listen as the teacher reads the book, and then the children seek out the book when it is placed in the reading center.

Some examples of books that might be produced in PowerPoint include *The Very Hungry Preschooler* as an extension of Eric Carle's (1969) *The Very Hungry Caterpillar; Apples on Our Heads!* based on Theo LeSieg's (1961/1989) *Ten Apples Up on Top!; If*

You Take a Preschooler Camping based on Laura Numeroff's (1998) *If You Give a Mouse a Cookie;* and *Friend, Friend, Whom Do You See?* based on Bill Martin, Jr. and Eric Carle's (1995) *Brown Bear, Brown Bear, What Do You See?* To create books like these, the creator might use images that are available from a clip art program in addition to photos of children. Since these books are pattern books, the creator is extending the pattern and personalizing it for the class.

The creator would begin with the PowerPoint Program. To open the PowerPoint program, move the cursor to the PowerPoint symbol in the dock. Click on it. (See Figure 9.18.)

Figure 9.18 Locating the PowerPoint Icon

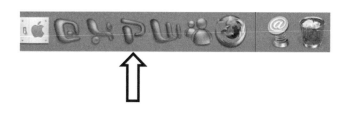

The PowerPoint program will then appear in the Toolbar. To start a new presentation, place the cursor on File. A drop-down menu appears. Scroll down and select New Presentation by releasing the cursor. (See Figure 9.19.)

Figure 9.19 Starting a New PowerPoint Presentation

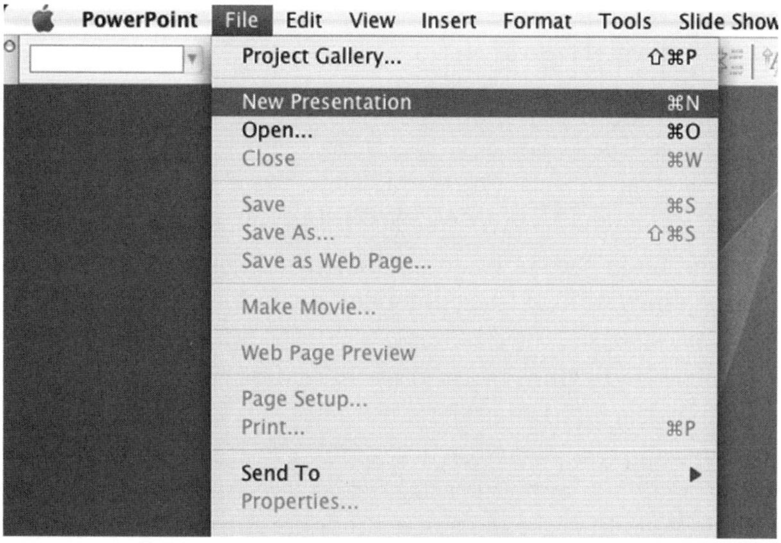

A new screen will appear that offers an array of choices for the type of page. Choose the Title Page by highlighting it by clicking on it. Then press OK. (See Figure 9.20.)

Figure 9.20 Choosing a Page Layout in PowerPoint

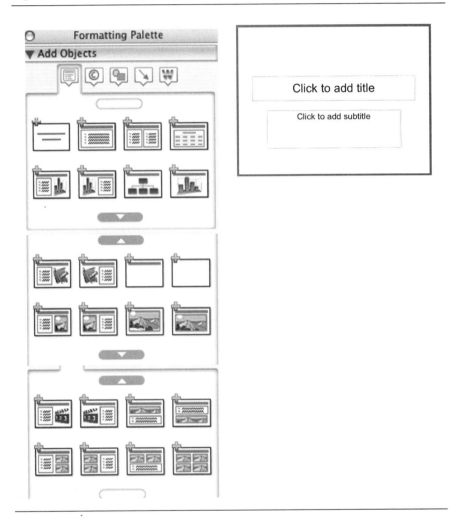

A Title Slide will pop up. Enter the desired information. To add additional pages, move the cursor to the toolbar. Place the cursor on Insert, click, scroll down to New Slide, and release. The New Slide page will pop up. Select a desired slide by scrolling down to one of the choices for "2 pictures & Text." Highlight it by clicking on the box. Then click OK. A new blank page appears. (See Figure 9.21.)

Use the Duplicate Slide function under the Insert command on the toolbar to create as many pages like this as desired. Develop the book by dragging in a photo of a child and appropriate clip art for the story; type in the patterned text. Remember to save often.

Figure 9.21   Selecting "2 Pictures & Text" slide

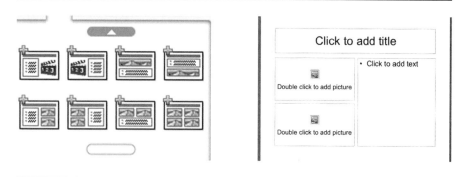

For example, to create *If You Take a Preschooler Camping,* brainstorm items that would be needed for camping: a backpack, a tent, a sleeping bag, a teddy bear, pajamas, a jacket, a flashlight, a campfire, marshmallows, etc. Enter the patterned text on successive pages. For example, on the first page of text, the script might be "If you take a preschooler camping, she will need a backpack." On the next page, the script might be "Then he would need a tent." Continue until there is a page for each child in the class. Drag in a photo of a child for each page. Then go to a clip art software program or a clip art Web site. Locate a desired image and drag it into the PowerPoint book on the appropriate page. Remember to save often! Repeat this process for additional clip art images.

Similarly, a PowerPoint book *Friend, Friend, Whom Do You See?* would feature two lines of text per page and one photo of one child per page, so the Picture Over Text option for slide selection would be desirable. For example, one line of text over the photo might read "Friend, friend, whom do you see?" and another line of text under the photo might read "I see Alex looking at me." The final page could be a class photo.

The "2 Pictures & Text" or "4 Pictures" slide selections within PowerPoint might be utilized to create *The Very Hungry Preschooler* (or *Kindergartner*) book. A photo of a child and images of food items would be placed on each page. To duplicate images, click on the image to be copied until boxes appear around the image. Then use the Copy function under the Edit command on the toolbar. Don't forget to follow up with the Paste function, which is also found under the Edit command on the toolbar. (See Figure 9.22.)

The text for this book might read "In September, Mika ate one hamburger each day, but he was still hungry. In October, Mika ate two hamburgers each day, but he was still hungry. . . ." Each month of the school year would be represented. Because the number of items consumed would increase on each page, the photos or clip art images would need to be duplicated as needed. As the number of duplicated images increases

Figure 9.22 Copy and Paste Functions

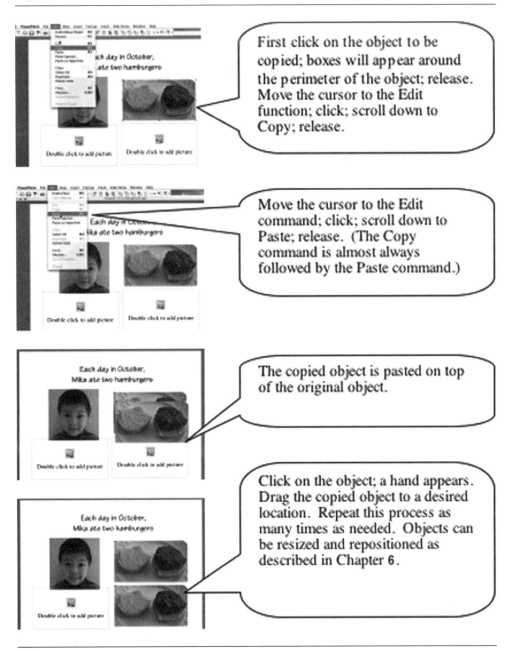

on each page, the image size may need to be decreased. (See Chapter 6 for how to resize objects.) The book concludes with the child enjoying summer vacation and returning as a kindergartener or first grader.

To create an *Apples on My Head!* book, one photo of a child would appear on each page. A clip art image of an apple would be duplicated as needed in this counting book. Manipulate the apple image to place it on

TEACHER STATEMENT 6

My 5-year-old son received a copy of the *Very Hungry Preschooler* with his pictures in it as a gift. He absolutely loves to read this book to everyone. The *Very Hungry Preschooler* book has given my preschooler confidence as a reader since it is the first book he has that he can read by himself. As a parent, I see that it has prepared my son for kindergarten. He knows that while kindergarten is coming soon, it won't come until after summer break. He has taken an interest in the calendar and the concepts of days, weeks, and months. This book is looked at on a daily basis by my son or daughter who likes to see her big brother's pictures in a book. The *Very Hungry Preschooler* is one of my son's most prized possessions.

—Jennifer Slipka
Parent

the top of the image of the child's head. The book might conclude with an image of a stop sign.

Other Story Stretchers might be based on folktales or children's songs, like "Mary Had a Little Lamb," in which many different animal images are invoked. Using the "We Have Animals" template provided on the CD, one makes a book in which a picture of a child appears on each page with the image of an animal. Some text could intentionally be left out for the children to practice language by using their words to describe the colors and textures of the feathers, fur, hides, fleece, etc. For example, the text might read "Ahmed had a little duck. Its feathers were as (color word or adjective) as (descriptor/noun)."

TEACHER STATEMENT 7

I created my own personalized book for children. In my preschool classroom, we were reading the book *Rumble in the Jungle* [Andreae, 2001], so I created a similar version of this book—only added in the children's pictures on each page. I chose to laminate and bind the book so it will last through many uses. The laminated pages made it easy to tape in pictures and take them off so that the same book could be used multiple times with different classes of children. The finished product was a hit! It looked like a professional creation and really impressed others. The children were thrilled to see their pictures on each page and would yell out children's names as they saw their pictures. It was a great way to work on identifying animals and other children in the class. The students enthusiastically participated and were eager to flip the pages. I plan to make many more books!

—Katie Deutsch
College Student

Creating Your Own Pattern Book

Beginning readers benefit from exposure to pattern books. A pattern book uses the same word string at the beginning of a sentence but changes the ending word to match the photo on each page. Some examples of patterns are as follows:

- This is a _____.
- I like to _____.
- This is my _____.
- I like to play with _____.

To create a pattern book in PowerPoint, create a title page, create a pattern page and duplicate it as often as necessary, then drag in photos of objects or people and type in the corresponding noun at the end of the pattern sentence.

Producing Your Own Theme-Based Books

Early childhood educators often utilize themes as a curriculum organizational tool. Thematic teaching is recognized as an appropriate brain-based teaching strategy (Brad Robertson, "Brain-Based Teaching," www.oct.ca/publications/professionally_speaking/september_1998/brain.htm), especially when themes are integrated throughout the curriculum and across developmental domains. Caine and Caine (1994) note that thematic teaching and integration of curriculum are two methods that teachers can use to facilitate brain-based learning.

Picture books that relate to a specific theme may or may not be available to add to a reading center or to use in Circle Time. When appropriate books cannot be found, books can be created using digital photography. For example, if the children are exploring workers, a relevant book to construct is one about the workers in the school, since they are a part of the children's daily experiences. This photo book features pictures of the teacher, classroom aides, center director, secretary, cook, janitor, and bus drivers. By using PowerPoint, one picture could be imported into each page. Blank space could be made available for the children to name and describe the work of the person pictured, or the teacher could supply the text when preparing the book.

> **APPLICATIONS IN A PRIMARY CLASSROOM**
>
> - Unit theme book: Take photos of primary-grade children as they act out their classroom themes. Make a class book about the theme. For example, one primary class was exploring the multiple intelligences, so they acted out each of the intelligences and then wrote a book about them that was illustrated with their photos.

Guest Visitor Book

When a visitor comes to class to demonstrate something for the children, make sure that photos are taken. It is wise to have the guest sign a photo release form. The photos can be made into a book to retell the story of this experience. For example, a woman came in to demonstrate the process of spinning sheep's wool into yarn, which is subsequently used for knitting. All of the children experienced the demonstration and could later revisit it through a class-made book (see Figure 9.23.).

Figure 9.23 Documenting a Guest Visitor's Demonstration

The Story of Wool

Ms. Mindy Rumkjr visits
Ready to Learn Preschool
December 1, 2007

Wool comes from sheep

Ms. R. showed us pictures of her sheep

Ms. R. showed us the fleece.

Fleece is raw wool.

Ms.R. used a handcard to comb the wool into rolag.

A Spinning Wheel spins the rolag into yarn.

This is the yarn winder on the spinning wheel.

Wool comes in different colors.

This skein of wool is white because it came from a white sheep.

Gray sheep make gray wool. Black sheep make black wool.

Wool is used for knitting.

People can knit socks, scarves, mittens, sweaters, caps, and afghan blankets with wool.

To produce such a book, use PowerPoint to import the photos and add text to tell the story.

Book About a Field Trip

When students participate in a field trip, be sure to bring the camera along to document the experience. Photos can be put into a book format so children can reflect on their experiences.

LOOKING BACK/LOOKING AHEAD

This chapter provided examples of how digital images can be used to facilitate children's literacy acquisition in the areas of speaking (for both English speakers and those who are learning English), listening, writing, illustrating, reading, and language arts. The next chapter will demonstrate how to use digital images in other areas of the curriculum.

Using Photos to   **10**
Create Curriculum
Materials

Digital photos can be used to enhance student learning in a variety of curriculum areas and centers. Books such as Susan Entz and Sheri Lyn Galarza's (2000) *Picture This: Digital and Instant Photography Activities for Early Childhood Learning* and Beth and Frank Geyer's (2005) *Teaching Early Concepts With Photos of Kids* provide many ideas for using photos to teach early concepts, language, storytelling, emergent literacy, self-awareness, social studies, movement and music, and cognitive development related to math and science concepts. A few additional ideas will be presented in this chapter to illustrate how photos can be employed in various learning centers.

USING PHOTOS IN THE BLOCK CENTER

Photos of children can be used to attract children to the block center so that they might work on block constructions to enhance their spatial relationship skills. When children see themselves as part of their constructions, they are motivated to play and learn in this area.

A popular book in many early learning environments is Wood's (1984) *The Napping House.* To extend this story into the block center, the teacher can take photos of the children while they are napping. The teacher prints the pictures in an appropriate size, laminates them for durability, and tapes them to the cardboard bricks that are often found in the block center. When children discover these bricks with their photos on them, they are motivated to build a "napping house."

Smaller images of children may be produced to tape to smaller wooden blocks. Be sure to laminate the photos to ensure durability. In this way, the images can be used as a prop in the block building area (Geyer & Geyer, 2005).

Taking photos of children as they construct in the block center also encourages children to play there. Photos might illustrate the rules for this center. For example, a photo could be taken of a child to demonstrate the rule of how high one might build with blocks. Another photo might show that four children can be in this center at one time. Other photos might demonstrate different ways to build with blocks: building roads, constructing enclosures for animals, erecting bridges, assembling villages, etc. A series of photos of block constructions could be displayed as a process chart to instruct children in differing ways of building with blocks. A teacher might create a block construction, take a photo of it from a variety of angles, and then put the blocks away. The photos could be displayed, and the children might be challenged to re-create the construction.

Photos might also be used to preserve the children's work when block constructions have to be put away. The next time that children want to use the block center, they can look at what they did previously and replicate it and build onto it.

Photos in the block center can also document children's cognitive growth by showing the children's constructions and how they evolve over time. Whenever using photos for assessment, be sure to date the photos so that they can be sequenced properly in a portfolio.

USING PHOTOS IN THE TABLE TOYS CENTER

Hands-on activities that use photos of the children will attract children to the table toys center. Creative teachers can look at the materials that they have in their centers and think about how they might create similar materials that use photos of the children. For example, a commercial product, Woodkins Dress-Up Kids (Drake, n.d.), has a full-body image of a child and some fabric scraps. Different, interchangeable facial images to depict diversity are included in this kit. The image is placed in a wooden sandwich board such that the area around the wooden doll is cut out on the upper part of the wooden sandwich. When a piece of cloth is inserted in the sandwich and the sandwich is closed, the doll appears to be wearing clothing made out of the fabric. If the center has this toy, it is easy to modify it to reflect the children in the classroom. Printing appropriately sized photos of the faces of the children and attaching them to the face pieces provided with the commercial toy would modify the toy to reflect the children in the class. In this way, the children can engage in pretend play as they dress their images.

To create puzzles, such as the one pictured in Figure 1.4, print large-size copies (8.5 × 11 inches) of photos of the children. To make the photos more manageable and sturdy, it is recommended that the photos be printed on sheets of magnetic paper. Cut the magnetic paper into as many puzzle pieces as are appropriate for the age of the children. Then set the puzzles on a metal surface (such as a cookie sheet) so that the children can construct the image.

Another use for photos in a manipulative center is to create sequencing cards so that children can order events from beginning to end. For example, when children are carving pumpkins in class, photos can be taken of the process. Photos of the pumpkin before it is carved, the lid being removed for interior scraping, the addition of facial features, and the completed jack-o-lantern will allow children to re-create the sequence later. Sequence cards can also be created to depict the changing of the seasons or the growth of seeds into a plant. To emphasize the classroom schedule, sequence cards can be created to depict the activities of the typical classroom day. Sequence cards can show how a child gets dressed to go outside on a cold day—putting on boots, then coat, then hat, then mittens. Sequence cards can be developed for any classroom activity that has a series of steps.

> **APPLICATIONS IN A PRIMARY CLASSROOM**
>
> • Sequencing: For children with special needs or children who benefit from social stories, create individual laminated books on rings that show the sequence of a daily routine.

Lacing activities promote eye/hand coordination and fine motor skills. When photos are laminated and holes are punched around the perimeter of the photo, children can lace around photos of themselves and their friends. On Valentine's Day, photos can be superimposed on hearts and then laminated; after holes are punched around the perimeter of the heart, children can lace around the photo to create a photo valentine sewing card. A "Valentine" template is on the enclosed CD. Drag photos into the center of the hearts, print, and then cut out the hearts and laminate. Punch holes around the perimeter to produce lacing cards. (See Figure 10.1.)

Create other seasonal lacing cards by downloading other seasonal images from a clip art program and then placing the images into the PowerPoint program. Insert the children's photos over the images, as with the valentine image provided on the CD.

Figure 10.1   Photo Lacing Cards

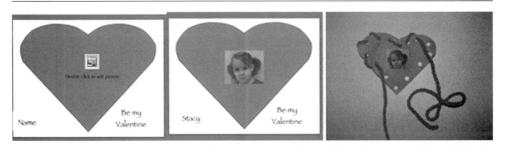

Additionally, creative teachers can use photos to create bingo games, concentration games, or matching games (as mentioned in Chapter 8).

USING PHOTOS IN THE CREATIVE DRAMATICS AND PUPPET CENTERS

Enhancing children's creativity is an often-stated standard for preprimary education. Photos taken of children can be used to record when children are engaged in creative dramatics or when putting on a puppet show.

Acting out familiar children's stories is one way to encourage creativity in young children. Familiar stories that are often used for creative dramatics include classic fairy tales like *The Three Little Pigs* or *Goldilocks and the Three Bears.* Classic nursery rhymes, such as *The Three Little Kittens* or *Humpty Dumpty,* are also appropriate for young children to act out. Other examples of creative dramatics might include acting out popular children's literature such as *Caps for Sale* by Slobodkina (1989). When children are performing, the play can be captured in photos, which then can be made into a classroom book. Or photos of the performance can be posted on a Parents' Bulletin Board or included in a newsletter. (See Figure 10.2.)

Figure 10.2   Photo of Children's Performance

Puppetry is another way to encourage children's language and creativity. When photos of children in the classroom are used to create puppets, the motivation to enter the puppet play area increases. To create such puppets, photos of either children's faces or whole bodies may be used. The photos are printed in an appropriate size, laminated, and attached to a Popsicle stick to create puppets (see Figure 10.3) (Geyer & Geyer, 2005). Create finger puppets by resizing photos to smaller images; sandwich a rubber band between the picture and the backing when gluing. Other ideas for puppet creation are featured in *Teaching Early Concepts with Photos of Kids* by Geyer and Geyer.

Figure 10.3 Popsicle Stick Photo Puppets

USING PHOTOS IN THE MATH CENTER

The National Council of Teachers of Mathematics has developed standards for mathematics education (http://standards.nctm.org/document/chapter4/index.htm). The standards include Number and Operations, Patterns and Relationships, Geometry and Spatial Awareness, Measurement, Data Description, Organization, Representation, Analysis, and Problem Solving. Photos of children can be used to promote these standards.

Number and Operations

This standard refers to concepts about numbers and how we can combine numbers through addition and subtraction. Photos of class members

APPLICATIONS IN A PRIMARY CLASSROOM

- Counting by 2s and 5s: Have children count photos in groups of two to encourage counting by twos, in groups of five to encourage counting by fives, etc. using attendance photos in a pocket chart.
- Place values: Have children count the number of photos of girls and the number of photos of boys using the attendance photos in a pocket chart. Discuss the number as it relates to the numeral in the ones place and the numeral in the tens spot.
- Numbers: Have children photograph numeral groupings of objects to construct their own photo number books.
- Operations: Create addition and subtraction cards with photos of the children in the class. For example, one card has a photo of three children on it, and the next card has a photo of four children on it. Children add to find the total number of children on both cards. (Cards can be created in PowerPoint using the 4 Photos Page option. When printing, use the Microsoft PowerPoint option of printing four or six slides per page to produce cards. See Chapter 6 for print options.)

can be used to pose problems related to this standard. For example, if there are 15 children in the class, the children could learn to count to 15 by counting class members' photos. The photos could be divided into photos of girls and photos of boys. Children could then count how many boys and girls are in the class. Children could then make comparisons to determine if there were more boys than girls or vice versa. Children could then become engaged in the operation of subtraction by finding the difference between the number of boys and number of girls. If photos are used on an attendance chart, children could routinely review how many children are present and absent each day. Teachers can create counting books, such as those featured in Chapter 9 that are available on the CD.

Patterns and Relationships

This standard helps children to recognize patterns as a prerequisite to learning algebra later. Photos of children and teachers can be used to create patterns. An AB pattern would require children to create a pattern of boy/girl or blue eyes/brown eyes by alternating the appropriate photos. An ABC pattern would require the children to create a pattern such as girl/boy/teacher or happy faces/sad faces/mad faces.

Geometry and Spatial Awareness

Photos of children creating shapes with their bodies can be made into a classroom shape book (Geyer & Geyer, 2005). Learning shapes can also be promoted by creating the Shape Book that was described in Chapter 9 and is available on the CD. Photos can be taken of children to demonstrate concepts of space such as "in," "on," "up," "down," "in front of," "behind," "under," etc. A playground photo shoot allows teachers to capture children in various spatial poses. For example, capturing a child crawling through a tunnel is a good example of the concept "in," while a photo of a child coming down a slide exemplifies the concept "down." The photos can then be placed in PowerPoint, and a book of spatial concepts can be produced.

APPLICATIONS IN A PRIMARY CLASSROOM

- Shapes: When studying shapes, have the children take photos of objects in the environment that are examples of shapes. For example, take a photo of a bicycle tire as an exemplar of a circle, a window pane as an exemplar of a square, a book as an exemplar of a rectangle, etc. Have the children make a shape book using the photos.
- Lines: Have children snap photos of exemplars of parallel lines and perpendicular lines in the environment.

Measurement

Young children are encouraged to practice measurement with non-traditional tools such as Popsicle sticks, string, and paper clips. The children's book *Ten Beads Tall* (Twinn, 1992) features illustrations of various objects and includes a string with moveable cubical wooden beads to use as a measuring tool. This book provides an inspiration for a teacher-made classroom book, as shown in Figure 10.4. Photos of children can be

Figure 10.4   Page From Photo Book *How Tall*

imported into the "Paperclips Tall" template on the CD in various sizes. The pages can be printed, placed in plastic protector sheets, and bound together with ring fasteners or placed in a three-ring binder. Paper clips can be attached or wooden or plastic beads that are available in hobby stores can be strung on a sturdy cord and tied to the book. Children can then be encouraged to measure how tall they are with the paper clips or the beads.

Data Description, Organization, Representation, and Analysis

Graphs can be used to illustrate a vote or to record children's data for a science experiment. When teachers create graphs, children can participate by placing their photos on the graph to indicate their votes. For example, at Thanksgiving, children might be asked to make a graph by placing their photos in the column under the food that they most like to eat at this holiday. Similar votes could be taken for favorite colors, seasons, activities, etc. At other times, children might collect data and put their results next to their photos. For example, children might estimate how many drops of water it will take to cover a penny, nickel, and dime. Placing pictures of the children into the math graphing activity personalizes the activity for the children. (See Figure 10.5.)

Figure 10.5   Graphing With Photos

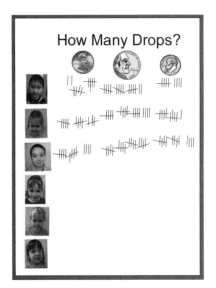
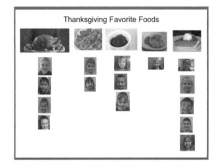

Problem Solving

Photos can be used to help young children problem-solve. For example, photos may be taken of children and the question can be posed: "How many napkins do we need to set out at snack time for these children?" In this way, children would practice one-to-one relationships. Or photos of children expressing different emotions can be made into laminated cards. Children can be directed to sort the photos into different emotional categories, thereby using classification skills.

USING PHOTOS AT THE SENSORY TABLE

The Sensory Area is a place for children to use their senses—particularly touch and sight. These experiences contribute to developing a child's observation skills, as well as serving as an emotionally satisfying experience. Often a sensory table or tub is filled with sand, birdseed, rice, beans, etc. Sometimes other items are hidden in the fill. Photos of objects that are buried in the sensory table could be posted near the sensory table so that children could dig for them and determine if they had found all the buried objects or not.

USING PHOTOS IN THE SCIENCE CENTER

To encourage children to choose independently to work in a science center, the teacher can scaffold the child's success by providing a process chart in the center. For example, a process chart for science would show, via pictures, the materials needed for an experiment, the steps involved in the experiment, and the expected outcome. The Dancing Popcorn experiment is pictured in Figure 10.6.

Figure 10.6 Science Experiment Process Chart

(Continued)

Figure 10.6 (Continued)

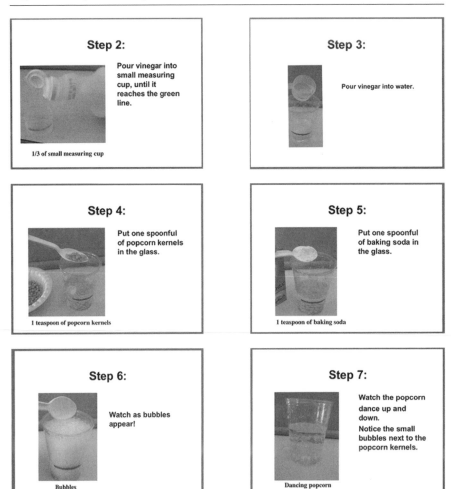

Observation is one of the primary objectives for young children as they explore science. To create an "I Spy" bottle, fill a clean, dry, clear water bottle with grains or seeds and place objects in it. Young children practice their observation skills as they shake the bottle and look for the objects. To challenge children to look for buried objects, take photos of the items and make a chart showing them. (See Figure 10.7.)

Another way to encourage children's observation skills is to engage them in a scavenger hunt. Each child is given a clipboard with a chart that contains photos of objects in the environment. As the children find the items, they check them off the photo list.

When doing sink/float experiences as part of the science curriculum, the teacher can help organize children's thinking by having children post pictures of the items in the proper columns of a chart. Pictures should be

Figure 10.7   Using Photos for "I Spy" Bottle

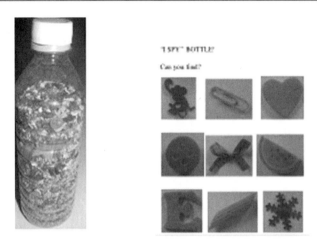

laminated. They can be attached with Velcro to a poster board or with a magnetic strip to a cookie sheet. (See Figure 10.8.) A similar chart could be made for magnet experiments.

Figure 10.8   Using Photos of Objects to Chart Results of Science Experiment

Photos may be taken when children plant seeds as part of a life science unit. A plant's growth and change over time can be recorded visually with daily photos. Observing a bunch of bananas over time is another activity that would encourage children to observe change. Each day, the teacher or a designated child takes a photo of the bananas until a sequence of photos is available. Children can arrange these photos as a seriation activity, from green to yellow, brown, and finally black.

APPLICATIONS IN A PRIMARY CLASSROOM

- Science Process: Create a sequence chart by taking photos to illustrate the steps in the science process.
- Science Fair: Snap photos to use on the display boards.

For more ideas specific to using photography for teaching science, please see Neumann-Hinds's (2007) *Picture Science: Using Digital Photography to Teach Young Children.*

USING PHOTOS IN THE COOKING CENTER

Recipe charts are an example of a specific process chart. Step-by-step directions are illustrated with photos, as shown in Figure 10.9. Recipes can also be illustrated for play dough or other sensory mixtures.

Figure 10.9   Recipe Chart for Ants on a Log

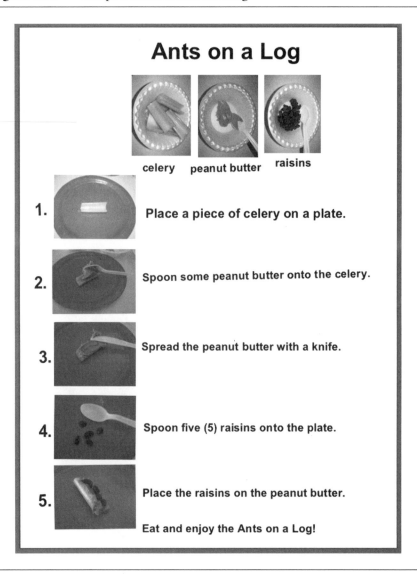

Using Photos to Promote Nutrition

Because of the growing concern regarding childhood obesity, teachers of young children can assist young children in making good food choices within their nutritional theme units. Using the "Eating Fruits" and "Eating Vegetables" templates can motivate children to focus on selecting more nutritious snacks.

USING PHOTOS IN THE ART CENTER

To enable children to approach an art activity independently, the teacher creates a photo process chart showing step-by-step directions for how to approach the task. For example, to illustrate how to do a crayon-release picture, take photos of the materials (a paint smock, paper, crayons, a paintbrush, water, and water colors) and photos of the process (draw on paper with a crayon, paint over the paper) and post the photos on a chart.

Photos of children can be incorporated into an art activity. In Chapter 8, an example was presented in which children completed a picture of themselves by drawing in their bodies when presented with photos of their faces on pieces of paper. An interesting adaptation of this application is to print the teacher's face on a page and have the children draw in the teacher's body (see Figure 10.10). This can be used as an engaging "Meet My Teacher" introduction at the beginning of the school year. The child's drawing coupled with the teacher's face photo can accompany a short biography of the

Figure 10.10 "Meet the Teacher"

teacher and then be sent home to the parents. Primary school children could be encouraged to write a story to accompany their artwork.

Photos of children can be incorporated into an activity around any theme. For example, if the theme is "flowers," photos of the children's faces are provided on pieces of paper, and the children are directed to make their faces into flowers. The face becomes the center of the flower, and the child can draw in petals, a stem, and leaves or use a torn paper/paste technique. If the theme is "insects," the children's facial images can be printed on pieces of paper, and the children will draw in the abdomen, thorax, legs, wings, and antennae of the insect using their faces as heads of the insects. (See Figure 10.11.)

Figure 10.11   Children's Images as Part of Art Related to a Unit

USING PHOTOS IN THE DRAMATIC PLAY CENTER

Through dramatic play, children learn about roles. A common dramatic play center revolves around the theme of camping. As part of camping, often the children are given props to go fishing as part of their pretend camping experience. Why not fish for friends? Laminate photos of children, attach adhesive magnetic strips to them, and give each child a dowel with a magnet on it. Children then catch photos as they fish for friends.

APPLICATIONS IN A PRIMARY CLASSROOM

- Perspective: Take photos of objects from different angles and different distances when introducing the concept of perspective in art. This can also be used as a social studies aid when discussing different points of view.

TEACHING SOCIAL STUDIES WITH PHOTOS

Teachers can create their own social studies books for young children when commercial products are not available. For example, when seeking books on the topic of community, it may be difficult to find appropriate children's books. By taking photos of familiar public buildings, stores, parks, schools, and neighborhoods along with photos of the "Welcome to . . ." sign for the community, the water tower with the community name, or the official highway sign with the community name and population figures, teachers can create their own picture books of the children's community.

When community helpers such as firefighters, postal workers, or dental hygienists visit the classroom, take photos of them and have the children dictate a story about their roles. Each visit creates a page in a book about community helpers.

APPLICATIONS IN A PRIMARY CLASSROOM

- Geography: When discussing a topic such as landmasses, create a class book by producing pages for each child regarding the landmass that they are researching. Each page would have a photo of the child, a downloaded image of a landmass, and then a few paragraphs of facts about the landmass (e.g., a definition of the landmass, what kinds of plants and animals live there, and an example of one such landmass).
- Geography: Create postcards of a place that children would like to visit. Include a photo of the child and a downloaded image of the desired geographical location. On the backside, children compose an imaginary story about the place.
- Geography: Create passports for children, as shown in Figure 10.12, by inserting their photos and information about them into the "Passport"

(Continued)

Figure 10.12   Passport

(Continued)

template on the CD. If desired, add a flag or global or other appropriate slide design background within the PowerPoint program. Place the cursor on Format on the PowerPoint toolbar. Scroll down to Slide Design. Choose an appropriate design. Check the box to apply to all slides. Then click on Apply, and the slide design will be added as a background to all slides. Print using the two slides per page option under MicroSoft PowerPoint when in the Print function. (See Chapter 6 for printing instructions.)

- History: Create a book about a class' personal history from the beginning of the school year to the end of the school year. Present a time line from September through June. For each month, list events that occurred in the classroom with photos documenting the events.

Another part of social studies is becoming aware of where one lives. It is common for young children to learn their addresses and phone numbers. The "Address & Phone" template permits the user to drag a photo of a child into the center photo box on each page. Pages include photos of single-family homes, apartment buildings, and mobile homes so that the user can select an appropriate representation of the child's homes. When the cursor is moved to the area of print, a text box appears, and appropriate information can be typed in. (See Figure 10.13.)

Figure 10.13   Page From "Address & Phone" Template

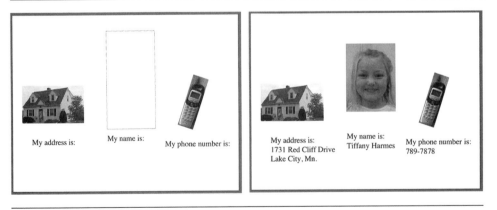

This book can become a flipbook if pages are uniformly cut into thirds, reordered to mix up the information, and then bound. Binding can be accomplished by punching holes in each section and placing them into a three-ring binder, or commercial binding machines may be used that use spiral binding. To ensure success in correctly matching addresses and phone numbers to children's photos, a self-correcting system of marking correct matches should be employed. That is, all three sections for one child could be identified with the same stickers on the back. Caution: Parental permission may be required to produce such a classroom book that discloses identifying information about a child.

Another social studies application is to use photos to tell social stories. A social story is a way to promote social problem solving or to promote desired social behaviors. For example, if a child with Down syndrome or a child from another cultural group is joining the class, the teacher might tell a story using the child's photo and photos of the other children. The storyline might revolve around how similar all children are, sharing common likes and dislikes, thereby focusing the children on shared experiences rather than on physical differences. The story would emphasize how all the children are friends in the community of the classroom. The final page would affirm friendships.

Multicultural awareness begins early with young children when teachers introduce children to greetings in other languages as a part of the curriculum. A "Hello" template is included on the CD so that photos of children can be paired with greetings from a variety of countries around the world.

USING PHOTOS FOR FIELD TRIPS

In preparation for a field trip, a teacher might show photos of some of the things that the children should look for on the field trip. For example, if preschool children are taking a field trip to a farm, they might be shown pictures of the animals, the farm equipment, and the farm buildings prior to leaving the center. Elementary children might be given a photo checklist of items that they take with them so that they can look for these objects and write a brief statement about them. For example, if children are visiting a science museum, they might be told, through photos, to look for the mummy exhibit, a dinosaur exhibit, a tornado exhibit, a five senses exhibit, etc. This photo assignment sheet will keep the children more focused and reduce the tendency of children to race from display to display without absorbing information at each.

As mentioned in Chapter 9, photos taken during field trips can be made into photo books. Using tools such as the "Trip to the Farm" template, "Trip to the Zoo" template, or "County Fair" template can assist children in remembering these field trips and integrating these experiences into literacy experiences.

Additionally, photos can be displayed in the classroom or put into a slide show to use as prompts when children reflect on their experiences. Photos can be taken of specific displays in a science museum. For example, photos can be taken of dinosaur bones and fossils while in a science or history museum. Children can then be given photos and do further research on the pictured item.

USING PHOTOS FOR TEACHER-DIRECTED ACTIVITIES

There are opportunities for teachers to use photos when leading a large- or small-group activity. Teachers may lead groups for story time (please see Chapter 9), music time, or circle time (see Chapter 7 regarding attendance, job assignments, and birthdays). Teachers may lead small groups to develop specific skills (examples such as matching games are presented in Chapter 8).

Using Photos During Music Time

Music time can also be a literacy time when song charts are incorporated into the routine. Children can begin to read the song if photos are included in the song chart so that children learn to recognize the song by the pictures. For example, if one is singing the song "Apples and Bananas," the song chart should feature pictures of apples and bananas as well as the lyrics to the song. If one is singing "I'm a Little Teapot," then a photo of a teapot should accompany the words on the chart. The song "Head, Shoulders, Knees, and Toes" can feature the close-up photos of body parts of children in the class.

Other children's music lends itself to incorporating children's photos as props for songs. For example, the song/chant "Who Took the Cookies From the Cookie Jar?" may be facilitated with a photo album of photos of children's faces. As each page unfolds, the chant focuses on that child as part of the chant. Of course, at different seasons, the chant can relate to pumpkins, shamrocks, hearts, etc.

A piggyback version of "Do You Know the Muffin Man?" is "Do You Know This Friend of Mine?" which can use the same album of photos (see the "Friend of Mine" template on the CD). Any song that features the names of students can also feature photos of the students. Photos can also be printed on pellon and used on a flannelboard.

If the class has children whose names are composed of five letters, the song "Bingo" can be adapted. For example, "I have a friend, she is a girl, and Molly is her name-o. M-O-L-L-Y, M-O-L-L-Y, M-O-L-L-Y, and Molly is her name-o." A song chart could include photos of the children as well as the lyrics.

The classic rhyme of "Ten in the Bed" can be further emphasized with Popsicle stick puppets of children in the class and a poster/picture of a bed. As the rhyme progresses, the children can hold their pictures as their photos are ousted from the bed.

Another use of Popsicle stick photo puppets is with the song "Twinkle, Twinkle, Little Star." Each child receives a Popsicle stick with a star on it; in the center of the star is a photo of the child. As the song is sung, children hold up their star photo puppets. The "Star" template is provided on the CD.

An alphabet book, like the one presented in Chapter 9, can be used to sing about children and the beginning letters of their names. This is based on *Sesame Street*'s "C Is for Cookie" song.

USING PHOTOS FOR GIFTS

Teachers often assist children in creating gifts for family members for holidays, Mother's Day, and Father's Day. Many of the ideas presented in Chapters 8 or 9 or in this chapter can also be used to create gifts. Other possible gifts include a calendar with photos of the children, a photo Christmas ornament (similar to the Photo Lacing Cards in Chapter 10), or a photo of a child printed on 8.5 × 11 inch cardstock paper accompanied by the child's handprint with a handprint poem (see Table 10.1).

Table 10.1   Handprint Poems Internet Sites

---

http://crafts.kaboose.com/handpoem.html

http://www.dltk-holidays.com/dad/mhandprintalt.html

http://www.dltk-holidays.com/mom/mhandprintpoem.htm

Another idea is to use a Popsicle stick puppet of a child that is inserted into a small clay pot of dirt. The children can decorate the clay pot with paints or markers. The clay pots can be displayed as the class' "Garden of Children: Growing and Learning." When parents visit for an open house or complete a parent/teacher conference, parents can take their special plant home as a participation thank-you gift.

LOOKING BACK/LOOKING AHEAD

This chapter presented many ideas for incorporating photos of people and objects into various learning centers, curricular areas, or gift ideas. The ideas presented here are just stepping-off points to inspire the reader to explore even more options for using technology in the early learning environment.

Part IV will address how photos can be used to communicate with parents and other professionals.

Part IV

Using Digital Images to Communicate With Parents and Other Professionals

A Picture's Worth a Thousand Words

11

Using Digital Photos to Communicate With Parents

Most early childhood educators are blessed with daily contact with parents. However, much of that contact is very brief as parents say good-bye to their children at the beginning of the day and then hello to their children at the end of the day. Since young children are not very good communicators about the day's events, it is necessary for teachers to fill in the gaps in communication. Additionally, teachers need to communicate about the program (schedule, activities, curriculum, etc.) and to report to parents about their children's progress. Sometimes it is desirable to communicate daily, sometimes weekly, sometimes monthly, sometimes only once or twice per year. On all of these occasions, it is possible to communicate better by using photos.

The Four C's of Communicating With Photos

1. Communicating with parents through displayed printed photos

2. Communicating with parents through printed newsnotes and newsletters

3. Communicating with parents through the Internet

4. Communicating with parents through slide shows on computers

COMMUNICATING WITH PARENTS THROUGH DISPLAYED PRINTED PHOTOS

Parent Communication Bulletin Board

Many early learning or care environments have a parent communication bulletin board either for the center or for each class. Typically these bulletin boards have a variety of things posted on them. The bulletin board might be divided into sections such as Menu for the Week, Wish List for Donations, Health Alert Information, Parent Meeting Notices, etc. After checking your center's or school's policy about publicly displaying photos, consider adding another section that says "What We Did at School!" or "Featured Children of the Week." This section could feature photos of children from the class or each class engaged in whatever they did that day or week. Perhaps a three-year-olds' classroom photo might show them engaged in dramatic play, a four-year-olds' classroom photo might show the children in a writing center, and an elementary classroom photo might show the children engaged in a project. Pictures could change daily or weekly, or different classrooms could be featured on different days. Because digital photography can be processed the same day on your computer, processing time does not delay using photos to communicate. It is very likely that parents would stop at this board daily to see what happened at school, as well as to see if their children were pictured that day. Another section could be devoted to introducing the teaching staff by posting photos of teachers with short biographies.

Some classrooms have bulletin boards inside the classroom, while others have them outside the room in the hallway. Take advantage of this space to communicate with parents about special projects in the room, a field trip, a special event, etc. When photos of children engaged in activities are posted, the photos communicate with parents. They also contribute to the children's sense of belongingness in the classroom. Children also enjoy seeing photos of themselves because doing so helps them feel valued, thus contributing to their self-esteem.

Displaying Photos on the Classroom Door

If there is no bulletin board, pictures can be posted on the classroom door, as shown in Figure 11.1, and changed daily or on some other regular basis. Occasionally, when there is a special event that would be nice to share with parents, post one or more digital pictures on the classroom door so parents can share in the event after the fact.

When parents see these displays, they have talking points to discuss with their children, thus promoting language development as well as nurturing the parent/child relationship.

Figure 11.1   Photos Displayed on the Classroom Door

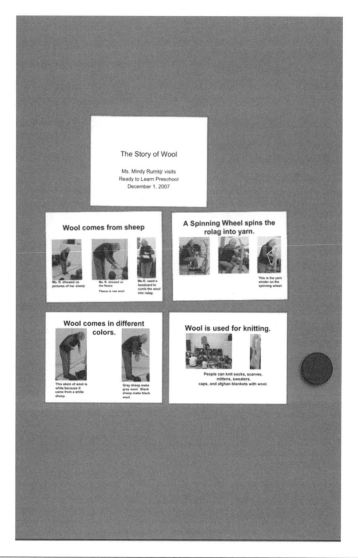

Printing Photos

After downloading the photos from the camera to your computer, you can print them using the computer's photo program. Photo programs vary; an example using iPhoto follows (see Figure 11.2):

1. While in the photo library, click on the photo until it is highlighted.

2. Place the cursor on the File function on the toolbar. When the drop-down menu appears, drag the cursor to the Print function until it is highlighted. Release the cursor.

Figure 11.2 Printing a Photo

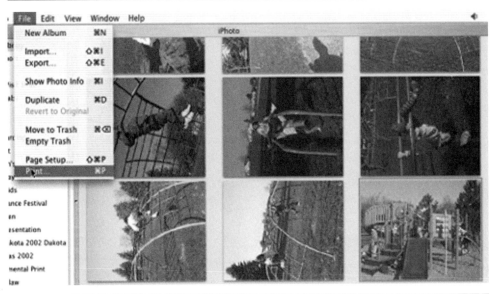

3. When a pop-up window appears, select the size of the print by placing the cursor on the up or down arrows; move the cursor to the desired size and then release. If more than one copy is needed, type in the number of desired copies in the appropriate box. Then press Print.

Other photo programs may have a print function within the program at the bottom of the photo files. Alternatively, photos can be imported into the PowerPoint program, as directed in Chapter 6.

COMMUNICATING WITH PARENTS THROUGH PRINT

Newsnotes With Photos

On occasion, teachers need to communicate brief information to all parents. At other times, teachers want to share information, but because of confidentiality issues, they want to communicate with only one child's parents; perhaps instead of posting photos on the door, a note is sent home with the child to convey a quick message about something that happened at the school or center that day.

Newsnotes can be sent to individual families or to all the families in the class. An example of an individual newsnote would be one that communicates about a single child who has achieved something special that day. Both the words and the photo communicate the achievement. A newsnote distributed to families of an entire class might feature photos of the class on a field trip that day or photos of a guest who interacted with the children or photos of a special party celebration.

One way to produce newsnotes is to use a Memo form from the Microsoft Word software program, which is found under the File options on the toolbar in the Project Gallery under Business Forms.

Another way to produce newsnotes is to use the "Newsnote" template on the CD that accompanies this book. Access the "Newsnote" template by inserting the CD into your drive. Click on the CD icon to open it, as you would click to open any file. Once the file is open, click on the "Newsnote" template icon to open the template.

When the file opens, you will see the template as shown in Figure 11.3.

Figure 11.3   "Newsnote" Blank Page

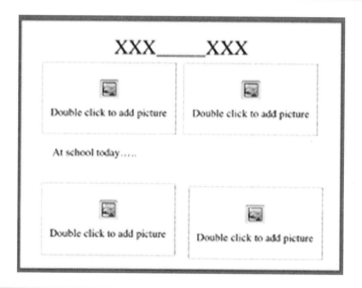

Highlight the XXX_____XXX by dragging the cursor over this text. Next hit the delete key on your keyboard. Now the title and date of your newsnote can be typed in this space.

To type in a brief message, place the cursor on the text "At school today . . ." A text box will appear. Now move the cursor below the statement "At school today . . ." and type in your brief message.

While the "Newsnote" template is open, open the photo file. Follow the directions outlined in Chapter 6 for importing a photo, moving the photo, or rotating the photo to achieve the right orientation within the PowerPoint presentation. Continue to drag other photos into the photo boxes.

If you do not want to include four photos, just click on the photo box until squares appear around the perimeter. Then hit the delete button on your keyboard. The box will disappear.

Save the newsnote by placing the cursor on the File function on the toolbar. Scroll down to Save As. When the pop-up window appears, give your newsnote a title, designate saving to the desktop, and hit the Save button. (See Figure 11.4.)

Figure 11.4   The Save As Function

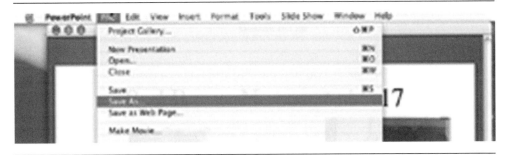

Don't forget to establish an electronic folder on the computer desktop in which to store the newsnotes. First click the cursor on the desktop (not on a file or while in a file). Go to the File function on the toolbar. Scroll down to New Folder. A new file folder will appear on your desktop. Label it "Newsnotes." Drag your completed newsnote file into the file folder. (See Figure 11.5.)

Figure 11.5   The New Folder Function

To print your newsnote, open the file that you want to print by clicking on its icon. You may now print the newsnote by placing the cursor on File on the toolbar, scrolling down, and clicking on Print. (See Chapter 6 for other print options.)

Newsletters With Photos

Many early childhood programs or primary-grade classrooms provide parents with a weekly newsletter or information sheet. Typically, the regular columns in this newsletter might include articles such as "Theme of the Week," "This Week's Very Important Kid," "Birthday People," "Menu for the Week," "Special Events," "Recipe of the Week," "Fingerplay of the Week," "Featured Children's Book," "Parenting Tips," "Parent Volunteers Needed for . . . ," etc. It is easy to include some photos of children as well as graphics from a clip art program. Photos and clip art are attention grabbers that pull the parent into reading the newsletter.

Designing a Newsletter Format on Your Own

There are many ways to construct a newsletter. It is best not to write a newsletter as if you were writing a typical letter of correspondence. Parents are busy people, so they don't want to have to search through the text for a piece of needed information. An alternative is to use columns and to bold the titles of sections so parents can find information easily. Another alternative is to use text boxes and include bolded titles within text boxes.

Using a Microsoft Word "Newsletter" Template

Microsoft Word has newsletter templates available. To find these on your computer, first go into the Microsoft Word program. Once the program boots up, locate File on the toolbar and click on it. A menu will appear. Scroll down to Project Gallery. The Project Gallery screen will pop up. Scroll down the column on the left side to Newsletters and click on Newsletters. An array of formats for newsletters will appear. Scroll down and select a format by highlighting the choice. Click on OK. The Newsletter Wizard will pop up along with newsletter page(s). Fill in the blanks. Select number of pages. Select number of columns. Save and exit.

Creating your own template from the Microsoft newsletter program involves deleting some of the examples embedded in the Microsoft Word "Newsletter" template. To form your own template, after deleting unnecessary information from the Microsoft Word "Newsletter" template, type in the titles of sections that you will use consistently. Save as "Newsletter Template." Once there is a saved template, information for the current newsletter plus photos can be inserted. Be sure to Save As "Newsletter [date]" so that your template can be preserved. Print and duplicate as needed.

Using the "Newsletter" Template on the CD

Access the template by inserting the CD into your drive. Click on the CD icon to open it, as you would click to open any file. Once the file is open, click on the "Newsletter" template icon to open it.

When the file opens, you will see the template as shown in Figure 11.6.

Figure 11.6   Blank Pages From the "Newsletter" Template

The template provides you with two pages so that you can produce a two-sided, one-page newsletter. However, you can choose to use only one side.

To use the "Newsletter" template, move the cursor to the top of the first page and highlight "Name of your Facility." Press the delete key on your keyboard. Type the name of your facility in this space; use the teacher's name for classroom news. (See Figure 11.7.)

Figure 11.7   Entering Data Into the "Newsletter" Template

Similarly, complete the other data points for volume, number, month/day/year, teacher name, e-mail address, and phone number (see Figure 11.8).

Fill in the boxes with information appropriate to each box. Remember to save often! Drag in photos as described for the "Newsnote" template. If photos are at the wrong orientation, rotate photos as explained in Chapter 6.

If you want to change the titles in the boxes, highlight as stated above and delete. Then type in your own title and complete the box by filling in appropriate information. Use the Save As function under the File function

Figure 11.8 Data Entered Into the "Newsletter" Template

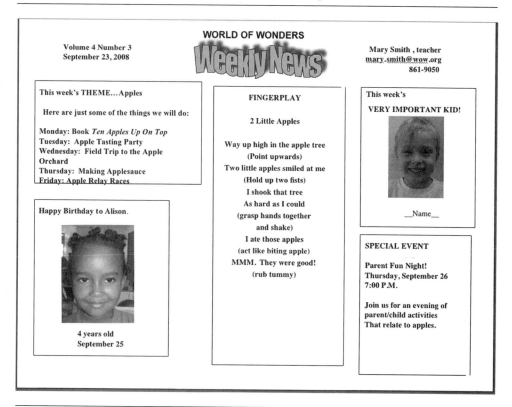

on the toolbar. Be sure to title your newsletter—for example, "Newsletter #3" or "Newsletter 9-25-08."

Store your newsletter in an electronic file on your desktop, using procedures similar to those stated for the newsnote file. There are two good reasons to save newsletters:

1. They are saved for future reference to make sure that you are not duplicating ideas within the same year.

2. They are saved so you can reuse portions in other calendar years. If similar themes are implemented in your classroom in future years, time is saved by cutting out old information, pasting in new information, and keeping standard information. For example, perhaps the same fingerplays are used, but a different child is celebrating a birthday.

Inserting Clip Art

Newsnotes can be more attractive if some graphics are included. (Please refer to Chapter 6 regarding how to insert clip art into a newsnote or any other product.)

COMMUNICATING WITH PARENTS THROUGH THE INTERNET

Sending Digital Photos via E-mail

An increasing number of educators as well as parents have access to e-mail. Sending a brief message with a photo attachment is another way to communicate with parents. This is essentially an electronic transmission of a newsnote. The advantage of sending photos via e-mail is that teachers don't have to spend time and money to print the photos. The disadvantage, of course, is that not all families have access to e-mail.

A consideration before sending a photo through e-mail is to change the settings on the camera to limit the camera's resolution to a lower setting. Michael Lawrence (2005) recommends setting your camera to the 640 × 480 size. Some cameras may label settings by file size, while others may have a setting for e-mail. Check the owner's manual that came with the camera for how to select image size.

It should be noted that some photo-file programs, like iPhoto on Macintosh computers, have a button at the base of the file that allows one to e-mail the photo. This feature prepares a photo for e-mail by changing its file size and automatically putting it into an e-mail message. The process is to 1) select the photo by highlighting, 2) type in the address of the recipient, 3) type in a subject line, 4) type in a brief message, and 5) send.

Computer systems vary as to how one attaches photos to an e-mail document. Some computers allow the user to drag a photo into the document. Other computers require the importing of an image as an attachment. Check the manual or Help function on the toolbar for your computer system for instructions for your particular setup.

Using Web Pages to Communicate With Families

Photo releases for publishing photos of children on the Web are required, because the photos on the Web are accessible to literally anyone in the world.

There are advantages and disadvantages to publishing photos of children on your program's Web page. One advantage is that parents, grandparents, and other relatives who have access to the Web can see photos of the children engaged in activities at school. This is a particular advantage for military families when a parent is stationed away from the rest of the family. It is also an advantage if international families have children enrolled in your program; these families can share their child's education with relatives who are living in other countries.

One disadvantage of publishing photos on the Web is that anyone in the world can access them. So if a family is concerned about custody issues, the family is unlikely to give permission to publish photos on the Web. Also, photos can be extracted from the Web and used in illegal ways.

Because of concerns about publishing on the Web, it is best to not focus on any particular child. Instead, group photos, photos taken from a distance, and photos that show activity but not faces should be the norm. It is advised that names not be attached to the photos.

A variety of Web page programs are available. Consult with a technician to determine which program best meets your programmatic needs.

COMMUNICATING WITH PARENTS THROUGH COMPUTER SLIDE SHOWS

Using digital photos of children in a slide show can enliven open houses or conferences with parents. During an open house, if the center has an LCD projector, teachers might put together a slide show to share with groups of parents. Another alternative is to have a computer station that parents can visit with their child. An automated, looped slide show could play continuously in this center. A similar slide show might be available for parents as they await their conference time.

There are some guidelines for preparing a slide show so that viewers will not be overwhelmed with too much information on each slide. For example, limit the number of words and the number of photos per slide. When using the slide templates, choose from the photo options. Limit the title to six words. For guidelines on producing an effective slide show presentation with PowerPoint, see http://mason.gmu.edu/~montecin/powerpoint.html.

A Slide Show on a TV Screen With Your Camera

The easiest form of slide show is achieved with the video-out feature of digital cameras, which allows a user to connect a camera to a television, monitor, VCR, or DVD player. Most digital cameras come with video-out cables so that users can display digital photos on common display devices. Video-out cables are typically distinguished by a yellow RCA jack connector that is inserted into display devices. Some cameras have an auto slide feature. Other cameras may require someone to operate the camera in the view mode and advance through the photos manually as photos are displayed on the monitor.

A Slide Show Using the Photo Program on a Computer

Another alternative for a slide show is to take advantage of the computer's slide show function within the photo gallery program. For example, the Macintosh iPhoto program permits storage of photos in files. To create a specific file of photos, place the cursor on the toolbar on File. Scroll down to New Album. A pop-screen will alert you to name the album. The album then appears in the list of albums on the iPhoto screen. Drag photos from the gallery into the album. If you want to move a whole series of photos at once, highlight the beginning photo in the series. Press the shift key and move the cursor to the last photo in the series. Click on the last photo. Lift the shift key. All the photos in the series will be highlighted. Place the cursor on one of the highlighted photos, click, and drag to the new photo album. A box will appear around the title of the album while the photos move into that file.

Some photos may need to be turned to the proper orientation. While in iPhoto, highlight the photo that needs to be turned by clicking on that photo. Look for the button with the rectangle and arrow under the list of albums. Place the cursor on this button and click for each rotation required to place the photo in an upright position. This process typically takes a little time, so be patient.

Once all the photos are in the album and in proper position, click on the album name. Then place the cursor on the triangle button in the controls below the album list and click. Your slide show will start and run continuously until you push the escape button on the computer.

A Slide Show Using Microsoft PowerPoint

Microsoft PowerPoint can be used to create a slide show that groups photos by topic and includes some text to explain the slides. To create such a show, open the PowerPoint program by clicking on the orange P icon on your desktop.

When the toolbar for PowerPoint appears, place the cursor on File, click, scroll down to New Presentation, and release (see Figure 11.9).

A pop-up window will appear with selections for layout, as shown in Figure 11.10. Scroll down to "4 Pictures." Click on it to select it. Move the cursor to OK and click.

A presentation window appears, as shown in Figure 11.11 on page 160.

Drag appropriate photos from the photo gallery into the slide. Resize photos as needed. (Directions for resizing are presented in Chapter 6.) Figure 11.12 on page 160 shows a completed slide with four photos.

Figure 11.9   The New Presentation Command on the PowerPoint Toolbar

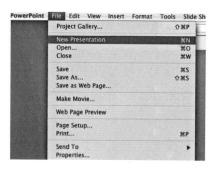

Figure 11.10   PowerPoint Slide Layout Choices

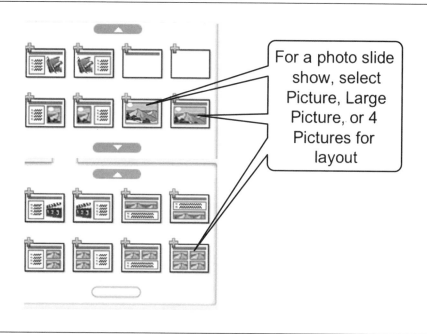

For a photo slide show, select Picture, Large Picture, or 4 Pictures for layout

Place the cursor inside the text box "Click to add title" and add some text to describe this page of photos. Save often during the construction of the slide show by placing the cursor on File on the toolbar. Scroll down to Save. The first time the presentation is saved, a pop-up window will appear in which you will insert a title of the presentation and select the location for storage on the computer.

To add additional slides, move the cursor to the Insert function on the toolbar. Scroll down to New Slide. A pop-up window will appear with layout

Figure 11.11   Blank Slide in Which to Insert Four Photos

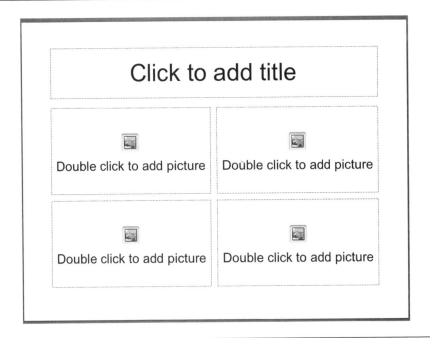

Figure 11.12   A Completed Slide With Four Photos

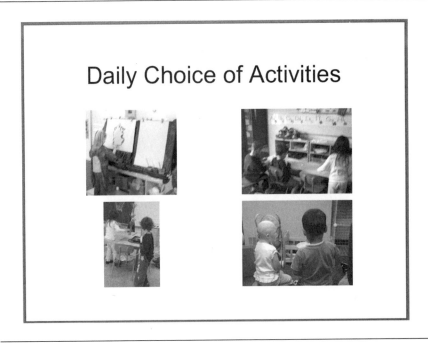

selections. Do as you did previously, scrolling down to select the layout of your choice, highlighting the choice, and clicking OK (see Figure 11.13). Another slide appears, and the process of inserting photos and text is repeated. The process continues until the slide show is complete.

Figure 11.13   Inserting a New Slide

To show the slide show continuously, move the cursor to the toolbar and click on Slide Show. Scroll down to Slide Transition (see Figure 11.14).

Figure 11.14   The Slide Transition Function

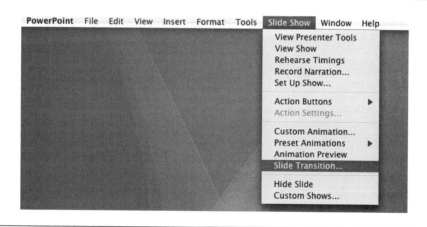

A pop-up window will appear (see Figure 11.15). Personal choice will determine whether a transition is selected or not. To choose a transition, place the cursor on the blue up and down arrows next to the box No Transition. Place the cursor on the box next to On Mouse Click. Click on the checkmark in this box to remove it; this allows slides to advance without a person having to click the mouse for each slide. Fill in a number in the box for "Automatically after ___ seconds." Typically ten seconds is enough time. Make sure that the box next to this command is checked. Move the cursor down and click on Apply to All. The setup window will disappear.

Figure 11.15   *Setting Up Slide Transitions*

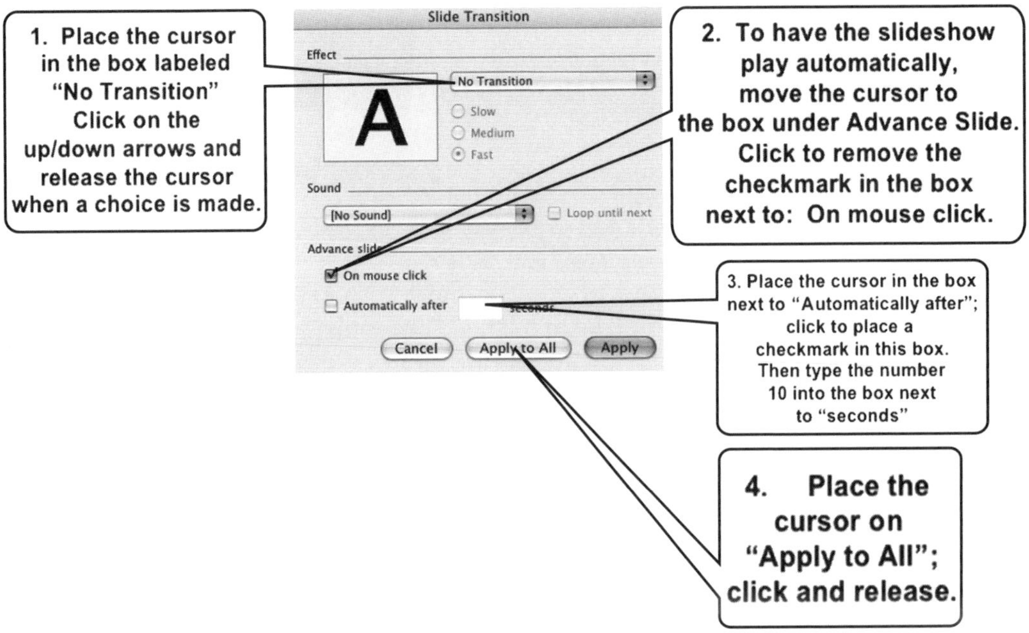

1. Place the cursor in the box labeled "No Transition" Click on the up/down arrows and release the cursor when a choice is made.

2. To have the slideshow play automatically, move the cursor to the box under Advance Slide. Click to remove the checkmark in the box next to: On mouse click.

3. Place the cursor in the box next to "Automatically after"; click to place a checkmark in this box. Then type the number 10 into the box next to "seconds"

4. Place the cursor on "Apply to All"; click and release.

The next step is to make sure that the slide show loops continuously. To do this, again return the cursor to the toolbar and click on the Slide Show function. Scroll down to Set Up Show and release the cursor. A window will pop up. As shown below, make sure that there are checkmarks in the following boxes: Loop Continuously Until 'Esc' under the Show Options; All under Slides; and Using Timings, If Present under Advance Slides. Then click on OK. (See Figure 11.16.)

To show the slide show, place the cursor on the toolbar on Slide Show and scroll down to View Show or click on the Slide Show button at the bottom of the PowerPoint slide (see Figure 11.17). To end the show, press the escape button on the computer.

Figure 11.16 Setting Up a Slide Show

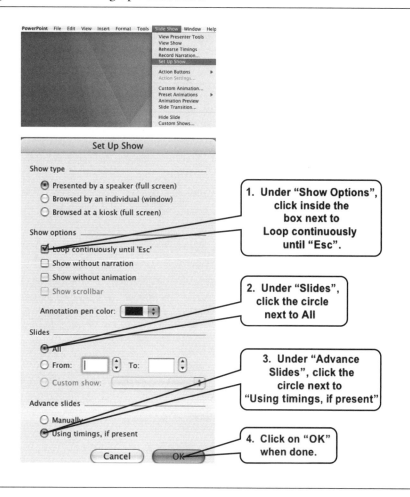

Figure 11.17 Two Ways to View a Slide Show

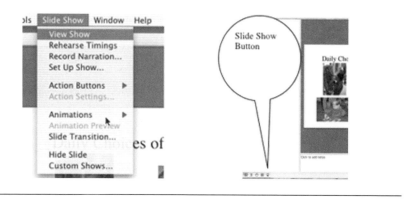

A Video Slide Show Using Pinnacle Studio

TEACHER STATEMENT 1

In Writer's Workshop, my students wrote reports about animals. After completing their report, they each painted a picture of their animals and I took pictures of each painting and imported them into Pinnacle Studio. After all the pictures were in order, I hooked up a microphone and had each child read their report as their painting was displayed. Later all the children were able to watch the video and learn about other animals their classmates studied.

We also created a Mother's Day video as a gift for Mother's Day. Students brought in pictures of their mothers and wrote what they loved about their mom. I placed all the children's pictures in the presentation and had each child read about their mother in the microphone. All the children decorated covers for their DVDs and cases and took them home as gifts.

To end the year, I created a presentation of our year in Kindergarten together. I gave each child a DVD to keep as a memory. The memory video was also used for next year's kindergartners to see as well as parents to view while they waited for conferences.

Pinnacle Studio is an awesome tool for teaching! It has been a great asset to my teaching and my students love to use it!

—Annie Tietz
Kindergarten Teacher

SOURCE: Courtesy of Annie Tietz. Used with permission.

A Slide Show Using Web-Based Tools

Several Web-based slide show programs are available. One such program, Smilebox, is available at http://smilebox.com. Follow the directions presented at the site.

LOOKING BACK/LOOKING AHEAD

The four *C*'s of communicating with parents provide guidelines for using digital photos, including displaying printed photos, publishing photos in newsnotes and newsletters, sending photos via e-mail or displaying them on Web pages, and creating a photo slide show for open houses or parent conferences. The next chapter will offer some ideas for using photographs to document children's development; these photos can be shared with parents as part of parent and teacher conferences and/or forwarded to the next teacher.

Picturing Growth and Development 12

Reporting Through Digital Images in a Photographic Portfolio

Assessing children's growth and development and, subsequently, reporting to parents about children's progress are important parts of being an early childhood educator. Primary-grade teachers report on children's academic skills as well as school behaviors. An assessment is evidence of what a child knows and can do. According to Mindes (2007), *assessment* can be defined as a process that can apply to an individual or a group that generates products and might be used for decision making. Assessments need to be comprehensive and address the whole child across all developmental domains. Mindes defines an appropriate assessment process as "systematic, multidisciplinary, and based on the everyday tasks of childhood" (p. 10). When working with young children, assessment should be authentic. This means that teachers need to catch children as they naturally perform or achieve a developmental task.

Teachers often rely on more than one form of assessment strategy to get a more comprehensive sense of the child's development. Some common assessment strategies include using state standards or developmental checklists, collecting samples of children's work, and observing young children. McAfee and Leong (2007) promote the use of photographs as an assessment recording procedure that describes pictorially. When a teacher heightens observation through the lens of a camera, observations become concrete products that can be shared.

PRODUCING A PHOTOGRAPHIC PORTFOLIO

The steps to use a digital photo portfolio of a child's development for reporting purposes are as follows:

1. Plan ahead for the types of photos that will illustrate the child's development or academic or social skills.

2. Plan ahead for when and where to take photos over the course of the reporting period.

3. Organize the electronic files on the computer so that photos can be inserted efficiently and appropriate text can be added.

Step 1: Planning for What Types of Photos to Capture

Typically, early childhood teachers report about children's progress in the developmental domains: physical development (large motor and fine motor), social/emotional development, cognitive development, self-help development, and language/literacy development. Primary-grade teachers document academic growth as well as behaviors within groups. Each teacher will want to develop his/her own checklist for each child in each of the domains or academic areas and select three or four items from the checklist that can be exemplified in photos.

Tools of the Trade: Preprimary Developmental Checklists

It is useful to have access to state early childhood standards or developmental checklists as guides to determine what to assess or observe. Most state guidelines are available online. Using search terms like *"early childhood standards"* or *"early learning standards"* will bring up a myriad of sources.

Many commercially available products provide information about typical sequences of child development for various age spans. Other resources are available online and can be accessed by searching for *"developmental checklists."* A sample of assessment tools is presented in Table 12.1.

Tools of the Trade: Standards in Elementary Education

Elementary education teachers are driven by state standards regarding what a child should know and be able to do at various grade levels. Since standards vary state by state, readers can locate their state standards at www.education-world.com/standards/state/index.shtml.

Table 12.1   Developmental Assessment Tools

Textbook
Allen, K. Eileen, & Marotz, Lynn R. (2007). *Developmental Profiles Pre-Birth Through Twelve* (5th ed.). Clifton Park, NY: Thomson Delmar Learning.
Assessment Tools From Nationally Recognized Programs
Child Observation Record (COR) from High Scope. Information about the COR is available at www.highscope.org, and it can be purchased online from this site.
The Creative Curriculum Developmental Continuum for Ages 3–5 is available for purchase from Teaching Strategies online at http://www.teachingstrategies.com/bookshop/ or by phoning 1-800-637-3652.
The Portage Guide: Birth to Six Checklists is available for purchase online at www .portageproject.org/brochure/Orderfrm.htm or by phoning 1-800-862-3725, ext. 221.
Assessment Checklists That are Available On-line
The Central New York (CNY) Early Childhood Direction Center has a free comprehensive checklist, which is available at http://thechp.syr.edu/checklist_download.html.
Another free source for checklists specific to various ages from birth to five is available from KidCentric Inc. at www.kcentric.com/Parents/DevelopmentalChecklists/ DevelopmentalChecklists.htm.

Selecting photographs to illustrate knowledge, skills, and dispositions. Having a checklist or list of standards as a resource can guide the teacher in selecting photographic moments that illustrate what a child knows or can do related to the developmental domains or areas represented in the state's standards. The teacher will want to select items that are appropriate to the child's developmental stage and then illustrate those items with photographs. Limit the number of photos taken in each domain to three or four per child per domain or assessment area. This is a reasonable number of photos to illustrate development and a reasonable number of digital photos to take of each child over a period of time. For example, if the teacher typically reports to parents twice a year in a nine-month program, the teacher would typically have approximately three to four months to gather a total of 25 photos, more or less, of each child to demonstrate growth and development in all the domains.

If the children being observed are four-year-olds, for instance, a checklist could guide the teacher to select photographic evidence of fine motor skills for illustrating development in the physical domain, such as holding a crayon in a tripod grasp, using scissors to cut along a straight line, printing some letters, and using eating utensils. Mindes (2007) states that photographs can be "particularly useful when recording sculpture, block designs, and group dynamics" (p. 86); these types of photos illustrate skills that children have developed. For example, photos of a child's block constructions can demonstrate that child's cognitive processes, and photos of a child's artwork can demonstrate fine motor and/or cognitive skills. The teacher would include these items on a photographic log sheet, like the one shown in Table 12.2, that includes the items to be photographed, the children's names, and the dates that the photos were taken. Logging dates is an important part of the assessment process, because change can be noted from one date to another.

Table 12.2   Sample Checklist for Photos in Preprimary Fine Motor Domain

Developmental Domain	Fine Motor		
Child's Name	Holding a Crayon in a Tripod Grasp	Using Scissors to Cut Along a Straight Line	Printing Some Letters
1. Blake	9–21–07	10–13–07	11–1–07
2. Chad	9–21–07	10–10–07	11–5–07
3. Demetri	9–23–07	10–10–07	11–3–07
4. Elena	9–25–07	10–11–07	11–4–07
5. Hamid	9–23–07	10–13–07	11–1–07
6. Irini	9–25–07	10–13–07	11–4–07
7. Jose	9–20–07	10–16–07	11–1–07
8. Kendra	9–25–07	10–12–07	11–3–07
9. Kyle	9–20–07	10–17–07	11–5–07
10. Lauren	9–21–07	10–10–07	11–3–07
11. Maria	9–23–07	10–11–07	11–3–07
12. Moesha	9–20–07	10–11–07	11–4–07
13. Rosa	9–20–07	10–11–07	11–4–07
14. Ryan	9–27–07	10–13–07	11–3–07
15. Wendi	9–17–07	10–11–07	11–4–07

This dated record will also provide data about when the photos were taken so when a photo is inserted into the photographic portfolio, the date can be added as well.

The photos in Figure 12.1 demonstrate fine motor skills, as well as eye-hand coordination. Similarly, checklists could be developed and photos gathered at other age or grade levels.

Figure 12.1   Photos to Demonstrate Fine Motor Skill Development

Step 2: Planning Ahead for Where and When to Take Photos

Where

Have a checklist ready with children's names and the checklist item that you want to photograph. It is advisable to place the checklist on a clipboard with an attached pen or pencil so that it is on a ready-made hard writing surface and the utensil is handy. Place this checklist in the area where the photo is likely to be taken. For example, the items listed above to demonstrate fine motor skills (holding a crayon in a tripod grasp, using scissors to cut along a straight line) are likely to occur in the art area, so the checklist should be placed in that area. When the teacher is ready to photograph "printing some letters," the checklist should be moved to the writing area. The camera should be fully charged with enough memory available to shoot the desired photos.

In general, fine motor skills are likely to occur at the writing center, the art center, or at table toys. Large motor skills are likely to occur outside or in the large motor room or gymnasium. Self-help skills are likely to occur in the locker area, at a sink, or in the snack area; photographing toileting skills requires judgment about appropriateness. Cognitive skills can be photographed in the block area, math area, science area, or puzzle place, and these photos may be of products as well as of children engaged in activities. Social skills can be photographed inside or outside during playtime or recess time to demonstrate friendships or dramatic play; social skills can also be photographed during group times when children take turns or raise hands. Language and literacy skills can be captured with digital images when children are engaged with books or flannelboard stories or when they put on puppet shows. Photographs of children's drawings and writing products can demonstrate illustrating and writing skills. Elementary teachers can plan their photos in appropriate classroom areas at appropriate times of the day.

When

The schedule of the day determines when getting appropriate photos will be easiest. For example, if large motor skills are being photographed, these likely will occur during outside time, large motor time, or physical education time. If social skills are to be recorded, these are likely to occur during playtimes, recess times, or lunchtimes. If photographs of self-help skills are needed, capturing a child getting dressed to go outside or washing hands before a snack are appropriate, so the camera would be needed at these times.

Because three of these activities typically occur in a writing center or art center, the teacher would know to be poised with a camera in these locations occasionally to capture the children as they naturally perform these tasks. Obviously, using eating utensils could best be captured during snack or meal times, so the teacher would need to plan ahead to have access to the camera then.

A checklist for an individual's Developmental Portfolio Photos was supplied in Chapter 5. To ensure that you are obtaining the necessary photos for each child, an individual record sheet provides all the necessary information on one sheet when you are ready to develop individual reports.

Step 3: Getting Organized With Electronic Files

After taking photos and downloading them to the computer, the next step is to organize those photos into files for easy accessibility. Establish a file for each child on the desktop or on a CD or flash drive. The file might consist of raw photos or an evolving PowerPoint presentation to which photos and text are added continuously as new data becomes available. Be sure to label the photos and date them.

Making Files of Photos of Each Child

To make a file of photos, place the cursor on the File command on the top toolbar of Microsoft Word. When the dropdown menu appears, click on New Folder. An untitled folder will appear on the desktop. As you click on the title "Untitled Folder," a gray box will appear around the title box. Type in the name of that folder—in the example in Figure 12.2 "Lauren." Continue this process until you have a folder for each child.

Figure 12.2   Establishing a Folder to File Each Child's Photos

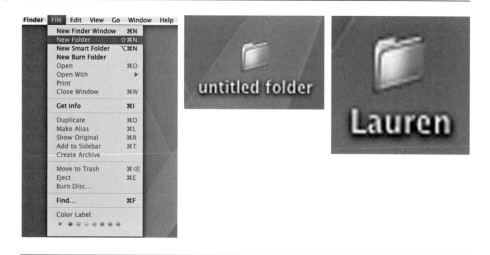

As the desktop fills up with folders, the final step is to create a final new folder to name "Children's Photos" with an appropriate indicator of the reporting period, such as "fall" or "spring" with the year (see Figure 12.3).

Figure 12.3   Master Folder for All Individual Photo Files

This becomes the master folder that will contain all the other folders you have created. Click on each of the other folders and drag them one by one into the master folder for desktop or other storage. When you double-click on the master folder, an array of individual folders will appear. (See Figure 12.4.)

Figure 12.4   Individual File Folders Within Master Folder

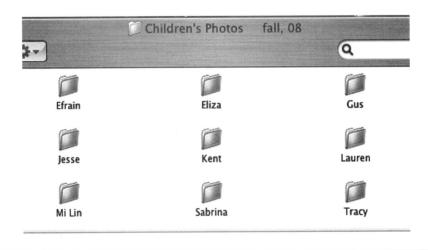

The next step is to put items into the folders. First, simultaneously open both the file of folders and the computer's photo album that contains the recently downloaded photos so that both opened files can be seen on your desktop. Drag the photos out of the computer's photo file by first clicking on the photo until it is highlighted, then placing the cursor over the highlighted photo and dragging it into the appropriate child's individual folder (see Figure 12.5). (It is best to get into the practice of automatically filing

Figure 12.5   Dragging a Photo From the Photo Album Into a File

photos after downloading each time to make organizing them a more manageable task.)

Repeat this process until all photos have been filed.

Filing Photos in Evolving PowerPoint Presentations

Another way to file children's photos is to import them immediately into an evolving PowerPoint presentation. The "Portfolio" template provided on the CD demonstrates how to organize photos into an evolving portfolio for preschoolers.

CREATING ELECTRONIC PORTFOLIOS USING THE "PORTFOLIO" TEMPLATE

There are three steps to filing photos in an evolving PowerPoint Presentation:

1) Creating templates for each child

2) Entering data into the templates

3) Sharing the portfolio with parents or guardians

Step 1: Creating Portfolio Templates for Each Child

An alternative to creating individual raw photo files is to drag photos immediately into the prepared PowerPoint "Portfolio" template. The benefit of this method is that you complete the task in one step instead of in two steps. Before dragging photos into PowerPoint, a portfolio file will need to be created for each child, as shown in Figure 12.6.

1) Load the CD that accompanies this book.

2) When the CD opens, you'll see a folder "Digital Images Templates."

3) Click on the folder. An array of files of templates appears.

4) Locate the "Portfolio" template file and place the cursor on it. While continuing to click, drag the file to the desktop.

5) The file on the desktop is a master template. Click on the title box and type in the name of a child, in this case "Lauren," to create a portfolio specific to that child.

Save the renamed file. Replicate this process, one by one, until there are enough Portfolio PowerPoint presentations for all the children.

Figure 12.6   Creating a "Portfolio" Template for Each Child From the Master "Portfolio" Template on the CD

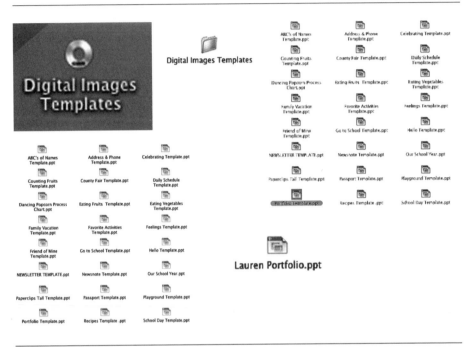

To tidy up the desktop, create a file in which to place all of these portfolio PowerPoint presentations. As directed earlier in the chapter, go to the top toolbar in Word and click on File. When the dropdown menu appears, click on "New Folder." Title the new folder "Portfolios (date)." Then drag each portfolio PowerPoint presentation into this folder.

Step 2: Entering Data Into Each Child's Portfolio File

Page 1: Title Page

This page serves as a cover page for the report. It identifies whose portfolio this is. (See Figure 12.7.)

Click on an individual child's portfolio file. On page 1, place the cursor where you see the *X*'s. Highlight the *X*'s by moving the cursor across them, releasing the cursor, and then pushing the delete button on the computer (see Figure 12.8). Next type in the child's name. Go up to the toolbar on the computer, place the cursor on File, and when the pop-up menu appears, scroll down to Save. Release the cursor, and this page is saved.

Place the cursor on the down arrow to advance to the next slide (see Figure 12.9 on page 176).

Figure 12.7 The Title Page of the "Portfolio" Template

Figure 12.8 Highlighting and Deleting to Insert Text

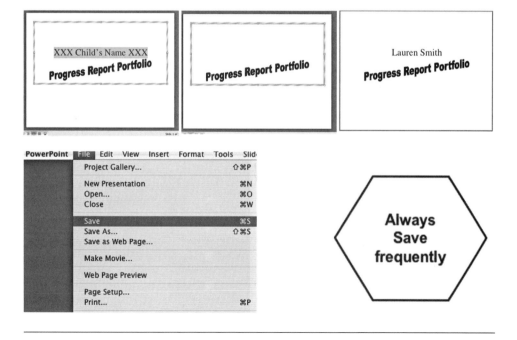

Figure 12.9   Advancing to the Next Slide

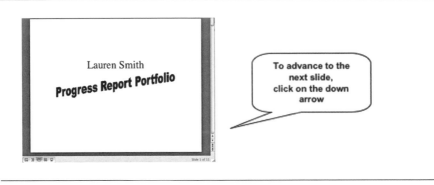

Page 2: Program Information

This page provides space for information about the program and the child's teachers.

As shown in Figure 12.10, drag the cursor across the "XXX Kindergarten," release the cursor, and delete. Enter the name of your program or class. Similarly delete other print on the page to customize to suit your program or school. If you choose to insert photos of the staff,

Figure 12.10   Entering Data Into Program Information Page of the "Portfolio" Template

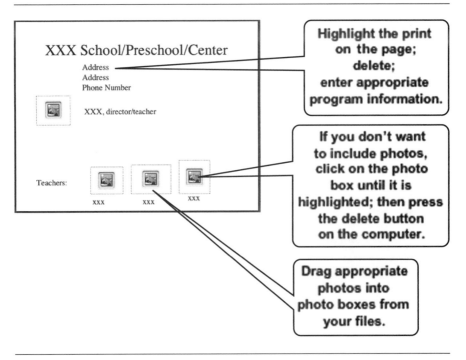

drag photos from your desktop files individually into each box. If you don't want to include photos of staff, click on the photo box until it is highlighted, then press the delete button. Remember to save frequently. Figure 12.11 shows an example of the result.

If you don't want to include this slide (or any slide) in the portfolio, when in normal view (see Chapter 6) place the cursor on the print to the left that pertains to this slide. When it is highlighted, press the delete button on your

Figure 12.11   Before and After Entering Data Into Program Information Page

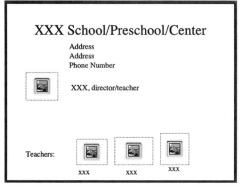 

computer. A warning sign will appear, and you can decide to continue to delete or cancel the delete command (see Figure 12.12). Because you always have a master template on your CD, you can always reload and start again.

Page 3: Child and Family Data Page

On this page, personal data about the child as well as the child's face photo can be entered.

As shown in Figure 12.13, highlight the XXX area as before to delete; then type in child's name. Type in data by placing the cursor where you want to start typing and enter data. To insert a photo, simultaneously open the child's photo file as well as keeping the child's portfolio PowerPoint presentation file open. Locate the child's face photo in the photo file. Place the cursor on the photo and drag it into the PowerPoint presentation (see Figure 12.14 on page 179).

When the cursor is released, the photo may fill the entire PowerPoint page. See Chapter 6 for directions to resize and reorient the photo. When the photo is in the desired location and all data has been entered, be sure to save! Figure 12.15 on page 179 shows an example of the end result.

Figure 12.12   Deleting a Slide From the "Portfolio" Template

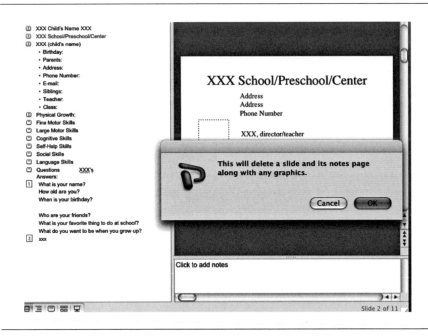

Figure 12.13   Page 3: Child and Family Data Page of the "Portfolio" Template

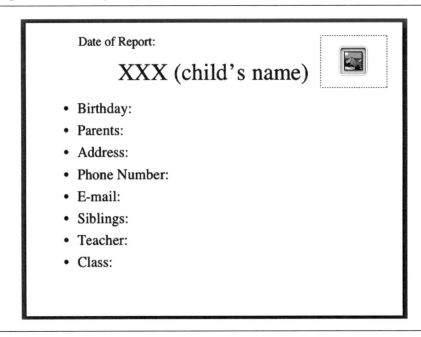

Figure 12.14   Dragging a Photo Into the Child and Family Data Page

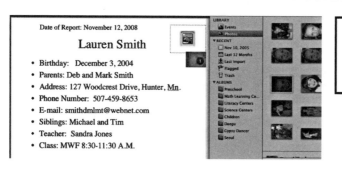

Figure 12.15   Completed Child and Family Data Page

Date of Report: November 12, 2008

Lauren Smith

- Birthday: December 3, 2004
- Parents: Deb and Mark Smith
- Address: 127 Woodcrest Drive, Hunter, Mn.
- Phone Number: 507-459-8653
- E-mail: smithdmlmt@webnet.com
- Siblings: Michael and Tim
- Teacher: Sandra Jones
- Class: MWF 8:30-11:30 A.M.

Page 4: Physical Growth Table

This page, shown in Figure 12.16, allows for the entry of data related to height and weight on three different dates.

To enter data, place the cursor in the appropriate cell and type in data. Figure 12.17 shows an example of the end result. Save!

Figure 12.16   Physical Growth Table Page of "Portfolio" Template

Physical Growth:

Date	Weight	Height

Figure 12.17   Data Entered Into the Physical Growth Page

Physical Growth:

Date	Weight	Height
10-24-08	57 lbs.	51 inches

Pages 5–10: Photo Reporting of Developmental Progress

These six slides, shown in Figure 12.18, allow for the insertion of photos to document a child's progress in the developmental domains of fine motor skills, large motor skills, cognitive skills, self-help skills, social skills, and language skills.

Figure 12.18   Pages 5–10 of the "Portfolio" Template

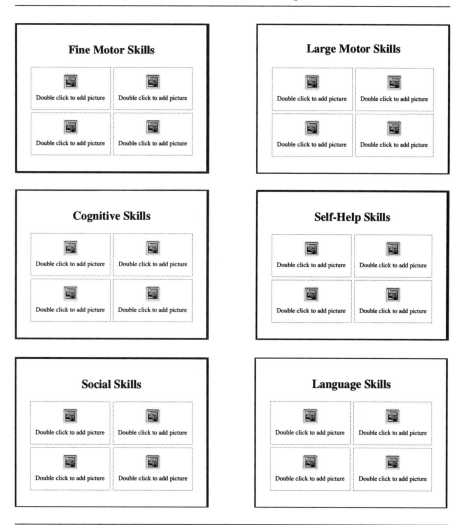

To add photos, follow the same steps as previously. Open both the portfolio PowerPoint presentation (to the appropriate slide) and the child's photo file or the computer photo album such that both are visible on the desktop. Locate a photo that demonstrates the developmental domain. Click on the photo until it is highlighted, then drag it into the PowerPoint presentation. If the photo fills the screen, do as directed earlier in Chapter 6 when relocation and resizing of the photo were explained.

Although a picture tells the story, further explanation of which skills the photos are demonstrating can be achieved with a brief written description. Additionally, photos should be dated. To add text, access the Text Box in the Drawing Toolbar or from the Insert command on the PowerPoint toolbar as directed in Chapter 6.

To access a text box, move the cursor to the Drawing toolbar and click on the *A*. When the box turns gray, move the cursor to the PowerPoint slide where you want to insert the text box (see Figure 12.19).

Figure 12.19   A Text Box Inserted Into the PowerPoint Slide

Once the box appears, text can be entered into the box by typing, as shown in Figure 12.20.

Return to the toolbar as often as necessary to repeat this process to continue to add text or to date the photos. Figure 12.21 shows an example of the end product.

A recording of the child's voice may be added to the Language Skills page to demonstrate mean length of sentence, use of descriptive words, etc. It may also be included to demonstrate that the child has articulation

Figure 12.20   Entering Text Into the Text Box

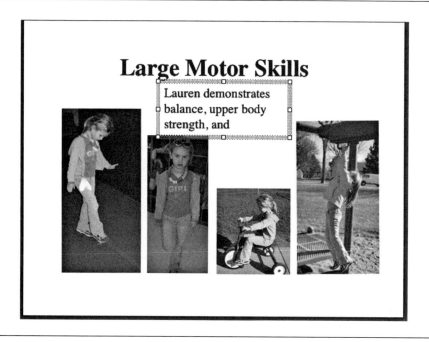

Figure 12.21   Completed Page With Photos, Dates, and Text

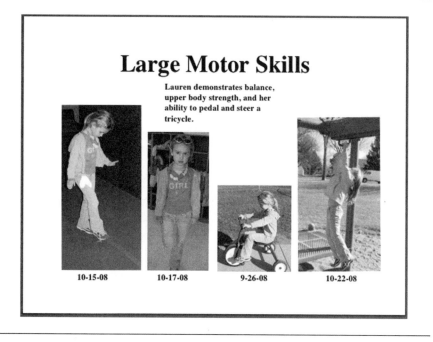

problems that might warrant a referral to special education services. A recording might also be added to the Cognitive Skills page to demonstrate the child's counting skills or ability to sing the alphabet song. (See Chapter 6 for directions related to the Record Sound function in PowerPoint.) Always save frequently.

Page 11: Questions and Answers

This data page, shown in Figure 12.22, allows the teacher to assess language skills such as mean length of sentence. The teacher can observe the inclusion of adjectives. It also gives insight into the child's social development.

Figure 12.22   The Questions and Answers Page of the "Portfolio" Template

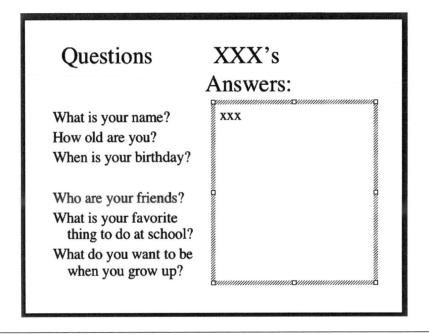

To prepare for completion of this page, the teacher should interview the child and write down the child's responses exactly as they are dictated. The teacher might also record the child's responses using the Record Sound function explained in Chapter 6, if the portfolio will be saved to a CD or shown to parents in a slide show during the conference. Once data is gathered, the teacher can enter it onto this slide. The large *X*'s on the slide should be deleted, and the child's name should be inserted. The small *x*'s should be deleted, and the child's responses should be typed in. If the teacher wants to change some of the questions, just click on that text box, delete, and type in other questions. When the page is complete, save!

Step 3: Sharing the Portfolio With Families or Guardians

There are three ways to share this portfolio: through a written copy, through an electronic copy in a slide show, or through an electronic copy that is saved to a CD and given to the families. The written copy will require printing. Slides can be shown on the computer and then burned to a CD so that families can have an electronic copy. E-mailing the portfolio is not recommended, since documents like a multipage portfolio with many photos take up too much space.

Printing

One option for sharing the portfolio is to print a copy of it. Pages can be printed in color or black-and-white. Printing color copies of multipage documents for many families can be costly. Pages can be printed in different sizes also. (See Chapter 6 for printing options in PowerPoint.)

Slide Show

To show the portfolio slide show, open the child's portfolio file. The show can be viewed by either (1) placing the cursor on the Slide Show icon at the bottom of the PowerPoint screen and clicking or (2) moving the cursor to the top toolbar to the Slide Show button, scrolling down to View Show, and releasing the cursor (see Figure 12.23).

Click to advance each slide as the portfolio is shared with parents.

Figure 12.23   Two Ways to View the Slide Show

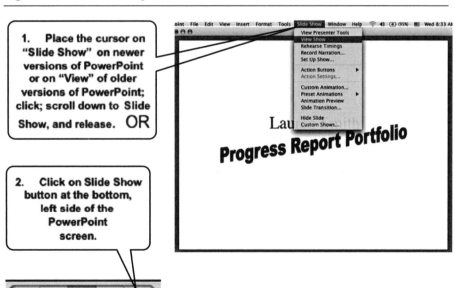

CD

Another way to share the portfolio is by burning a copy of the portfolio file to a compact disk. Insert a blank CD-R disk into the disk drive. When it appears on the screen, title it. Drag the portfolio file to the CD icon. When it is finished copying to the CD, burn the CD using the procedures that are indicated for the computer. When this process is complete, be sure to label the CD with an indelible marker or by using labels specifically made for CDs.

OTHER USES OF THE ELECTRONIC PORTFOLIO

Once an electronic portfolio has been established for a child, it is easy to add to it over time, thus providing a longitudinal record of a child's progress. If permissions are obtained from parents, the electronic portfolio can be included in the child's records when the child transfers schools or progresses from teacher to teacher. McAfee and Leong (2007) state that "the long-term storage and tracking possibilities could be useful for following children's progress from one grade or school to the next" (p. 113).

LOOKING BACK/LOOKING AHEAD

This chapter offered guidance to teachers with regards to developing photographic portfolios to use as part of their documentation when reporting to parents. These photographic portfolios can also be shared with the child's next teacher. The final part of this book consists of one chapter that presents some ideas for other uses of digital photos with children, families, and staff.

Part V

Other Uses for Digital Images in Early Education

Other Uses for Digital Images With Children, Families, and Staff

13

U sing digital photography is not just limited to teachers in the classroom. Children, parents, and other staff members can also use the rationale, tips, and tools presented in Chapters 1–6. This chapter will launch others to use digital images in a variety of ways.

CHILDREN USING CAMERAS

Digital photography is so user-friendly that even a child can do it. However, for obvious reasons, inexpensive digital cameras should be sought for children to use. Although some commercially made cameras are marketed for children's use, one should be careful to purchase cameras that are large enough but not too large and heavy for a child to manipulate easily. A minimum number of features is required when a child uses a camera. Point-and-shoot cameras with LCD viewfinders on the back are easy for children to use. Camera straps protect the cameras from being dropped; camera straps that can be worn around the neck are more secure than wrist straps. More and more manufacturers are producing kid-friendly cameras. Before purchasing cameras for children, consult the Internet using a search for *"digital cameras" children* as well as for *beginner "digital cameras."* Some sites to consult are listed in Table 13.1.

When children use cameras, they need some directions. Do not assume that children have been exposed to cameras before. First of all, children need to be instructed that the camera is a tool, not a toy, and needs to be respected. Much of the training will need to be done on a one-to-one basis.

Table 13.1   Sites for Information About Children's Digital Cameras

http://cameras.about.com/od/digitalcameragifts/tp/camerasforkids.htm

http://holidays.about.com/od/giftsforkids/tp/camerasforkids.htm

Children need to be shown some very basic safety procedures for handling the camera. A useful source that outlines instructions for children about digital cameras can be found at www.youthlearn.org/learning/activities/multimedia/photo1.asp.

Children should be shown how to place the camera strap on their wrists or over their heads to ensure that the camera will not be dropped. Second, children need some instruction in how to hold the camera, how to turn the camera on for use and off when not in use, where the shutter button is, and how to use the viewfinder to focus on the object or event to be photographed. A demonstration of centering the object or event in the viewfinder will lead to more successful outcomes. Because children love to look at the photos, they should be shown how to review the photo on the viewfinder once it has been taken. Although you might demonstrate how to delete photos, this is not a necessary function for young children; you can delete unwanted photos with the child. If the camera has a lens cap, children should be told to protect the lens with its cover.

Children also need to be cautioned about privacy issues and about asking permission to take photos; informed consent forms for children using cameras in the classroom are presented in Chapter 3.

Once children have gone through training and can demonstrate their understanding of proper use and care of a camera, they can be given a photographer's certificate with their picture on the front and rules for camera use printed on the back (www.wacona.com/digicam/digicam.html). For a list of books on digital photography for children, see Table 13.2.

Table 13.2   Digital Photography Books for Children

Bidner, Jenni. (2004). *The kid's guide to digital photography: How to shoot, save, play with & print your digital photos.* Asheville, NC: Lark Books.

Digital photography for kids (kids essentials). (2006). Northamptonshire, United Kingdom: Igloo Books.

Ewald, Wendy, & Lightfoot, Alexandra. (2003). *I wanna take me a picture: Teaching photography and writing to children.* Boston: Beacon Press.

Friedman, Debra. (2003). *Picture this: Fun photography and crafts (kids can do it).* Tonawanda, NY: Kids Can Press.

Because it is unlikely that enough cameras will be available for all the children at once, it is necessary to clearly state (with a chart) whose turn it will be and for how long. The duration of camera use might be stated in minutes. For example, during choice time in a preschool or kindergarten setting, there might be a Photography Center, so children could check in and out of this center. Children who participate in this center would have the camera for ten minutes or so and could capture their peers working in other centers. (Setting a timer that alerts children to the end of their turns with a visible countdown digital clock and/or an auditory sound helps to avoid disputes.) If the typical one-hour of choice time is available, approximately four children could use the camera each day. In this way, in a typical class of 15–20 children, each child would have the opportunity to use the camera each week.

Another possibility is to assign a child to be the class photographer for an event, such as when a guest speaker visits the class. A third option is that the job of photographer be one of the assigned daily jobs that is rotated among all the children.

Depending upon the size of the memory storage for the children's camera, the teacher might need to download photos to the computer after each child has a turn. If the camera has larger memory, the photos might be downloaded at the end of the day.

The teacher may also consider assisting children using cameras in thinking about what they want to capture in a picture instead of just randomly snapping away. Teachers might sit down with children and brainstorm some items or events that would be interesting to photograph. Writing down their ideas on chart paper can make a quick reference resource when children need reminders.

Children's photos are a form of art, so it is important that this artwork is displayed. Be sure to designate a bulletin board as the showcase for children's photos. When teachers engage the children in describing their photos, they are fostering communication. When teachers write down the children's descriptions and post them next to the photos, emergent literacy is enhanced. When parents view the bulletin board with the captions, they gain a better sense of the classroom experiences in which their children engage. Another way of highlighting the photos is to include a discussion about them during Show and Share time. In this way, young children learn about turn taking, talking, and listening while showing off their works of art.

There are benefits to children using cameras. One benefit is that children's photos give teachers insights into what is important to children. Another benefit is that children can practice better observation skills as they focus on their subjects. Finally, when children see their photos displayed, they beam with pride!

FAMILIES AND DIGITAL PHOTOGRAPHY

Families can use digital photography as a parent involvement activity with their children, or they can use digital images for their own family records.

"Take Home Snappy"

Some preschool, kindergarten, and primary classrooms have included a take-home parent/child activity that involves the children taking turns bringing home a bag that contains a stuffed animal along with a journal. At the conclusion of the stuffed animal's visit to the child's home, the young child dictates the story of what the stuffed animal did to the parent; older children write their own stories. Sometimes the child is encouraged to illustrate the story. The children are expected to sign their entries in the journal. When the child returns the bag with the stuffed animal and journal to school, time is spent sharing the stuffed animal's adventures with the other students. In this way, the children practice many emergent literacy skills: speaking while dictating the story, listening while the story is read to the class, illustrating the story, writing their names, and getting practice in linking print to the spoken word.

Similarly, instead of a stuffed animal, a bag with an inexpensive digital camera might be sent home with the children. It could be labeled "Take Home Snappy." Children would be encouraged to take photos of something that they want to share with their friends at school. Or the camera could be paired with the stuffed animal so that the child can take photos of the stuffed animal engaged in some activity. A journal would be provided for the child-to-parent dictation. When the child returns the camera to school, the teacher downloads the photos and prints one or two of the photos that the child wants to discuss. The child's photos are then posted on a bulletin board along with those of their peers to document the adventures of "Take Home Snappy."

Because cameras are tools and require care and safety in use, some rules need to be presented in writing to parents early in the school year. Parents would need to agree to replace the camera if it is lost or broken. If parents decline their child's participation at home, the children could contribute photos taken at school.

Producing Family Books

Families have documented birthdays, holidays, vacations, and other special occasions using traditional photo albums. (See the examples in Figures 13.1 and 13.2.) In this technological age, those albums can be created digitally using programs such as PowerPoint to organize photos and include some text to describe the events. Two templates, Celebrating and Family Vacation, are provided on the CD that can be used to produce special memory books for families.

Figure 13.1   A Family Celebration Book

Figure 13.2   A Family Vacation Book

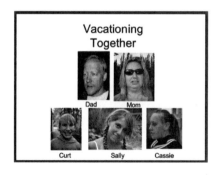

DIGITAL IMAGE USES BY AND FOR STAFF

A picture is worth a thousand words, so photos can be used to enhance communication with substitute teachers and other staff members. When a substitute teacher is called in, photos can be invaluable aids. A three-ring binder with sheet protectors can be prepared as a Substitute Teacher Book such that current information is provided through photo images. In addition to the photo attendance charts, previously mentioned in Chapter 7, there might be a photo seating chart for the primary-grade classroom. Photos of special procedures or materials can be helpful for substitute teachers. Additionally, photos of other staff members who are in the classroom throughout the day can assist the substitute teacher with knowing who will be in the classroom at what time and for what purpose.

If there are specific ways to use certain curriculum materials (Montessori equipment, for example), photos of the materials as well as the written sequence to be followed in their use could be developed for staff training manuals. Photos can be used to create process charts for staff to demonstrate how to use different forms of technology. For example, a sequence of photos can show how to send a fax or how to use the laminating machine.

Snapping photos of the classroom environment and bulletin boards throughout the year can serve as a record of themes, room arrangements, and projects. This documentation can become a resource to staff members in the future.

Sometimes when there are children with special needs in the classroom, teachers or staff members are asked to complete physical therapy exercises or to implement some occupational therapy experiences. While the therapists may demonstrate the exercises or give handouts that show diagrams about how to do the exercises, seeing sequences of photos of the therapist doing the exercises with the child reassures the typically trained teacher or staff member of his or her ability to follow through.

Teachers are sometimes seen at professional development conferences with digital cameras in hand. Taking photos of displays or of objects in make-it/take-it workshops preserves ideas and saves the time of writing down details that need to be remembered to replicate good ideas.

USING PHOTOS FOR FUNDRAISING PROJECTS

Most schools need to solicit additional financial support through fundraising efforts. Digital photography can assist with these efforts. Photos of children can be used to create books that parents or grandparents might be interested in purchasing. Photos of children can also be printed on cloth and made into T-shirts or a quilt. In addition to assisting with fundraising, these highly visible products are good publicity for programs and schools.

Recipe Book

A book that might be created to use as a fundraiser is a recipe book. A template for children's recipes, provided on the accompanying CD, is shown in Figure 13.3.

Figure 13.3   The "Children's Recipes" Template

Recipes Template .ppt

The "Children's Recipes" template allows the user to drag in a photo of the child and import a clip art image of a food item. Prior to publishing the book, the child should be solicited for a recipe for his/her favorite food. The recipe should be written just as it is dictated. For example, if the child says to cook a turkey for three minutes in the microwave, that is what is typed into the text. The user deletes the X's and replaces them with the child's name. The Z's are deleted and replaced with the name of the food. The recipe is typed in the space labeled "Recipe goes here." (See Figure 13.4.) Twenty pages are available in the template so that 20 children can contribute recipes. (If more pages are needed, use the Duplicate function as described in Chapter 6.) Save your work often.

Figure 13.4   Pages From the "Children's Recipes" Template

Because printing in color is time consuming and costly, the user may want to print the majority of the pages in black-and-white. Consult with a commercial printing business about duplicating and binding the book.

Yearbook

Just as high schools often produce yearbooks, an early learning center or school might produce a yearbook as a fundraiser. Photos of each child, each class, children celebrating birthdays, children who are "Very Important Kids" or "Stars of the Week," children engaged in play, guest speakers or guest performers, field trips, and parent nights could be featured. A yearbook requires careful planning and the systematic acquisition of appropriate photos. This is another opportunity to use classroom record keeping, as mentioned in Chapter 5. It is important to have parental permission to take photos and publish them in a yearbook that can be sold. It is also important to represent the population of the class or school fairly with equal numbers of photos of each child.

A "Yearbook" template, shown in Figure 13.5, is supplied on the enclosed CD. The template consists of the following pages: title page, class membership page, class portrait page, monthly birthday pages, "Very Important Kid" pages, monthly activities pages, and other pages.

Figure 13.5   "Yearbook" Template

Yearbook Template.ppt

Title Page

This page, shown in Figure 13.6, is designed for the user to insert a photo of the outside of the school building or the school's sign or a scanned image of the school's logo. When the user clicks on the box with the X's, the user can delete the X's using the delete button on the computer; the name of the center can be typed in.

Figure 13.6   The Title Page From the "Yearbook" Template: Before and After Entering Data

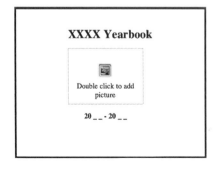
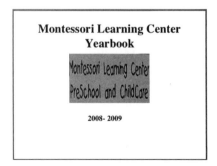

SOURCE: Montessori Learning Center—photo of sign and slides courtesy of Linda Good. Used with permission.

In the box that contains the dates of the school year, the user can delete the underlining by using the delete button on the computer and then fill in the numerals for the appropriate school year. Use the Save As function to begin to save the emerging yearbook to the desktop.

The Class Membership Page

This page is designed to show individual photos of each child as a member of the class (see Figure 13.7). Click on the text box, delete the *X*'s, and replace them with the class name. Drag photos of class members into the boxes; this may require resizing and rotation (see Chapter 6). Additionally, to add names, it is necessary to use the Text Box function on the drawing toolbar as described in Chapter 6. In the text box, the font size will likely need to be reduced, since the standard font size is 24 and a smaller font (size 12 or 14) is desirable here. To change the font size, highlight the typing, place the cursor on the Format command on the PowerPoint toolbar, scroll down to Font, and release the cursor. A pop-up window will appear, and a font size can be selected by scrolling in the appropriate box or by typing in the numeral in the box (see Figure 13.8). Save.

Figure 13.7   The Class Membership Page From the "Yearbook" Template

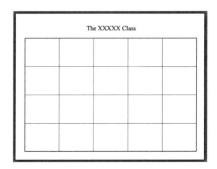 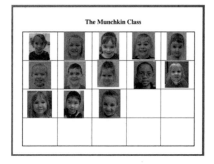

Figure 13.8   Two Ways to Select a Font Size

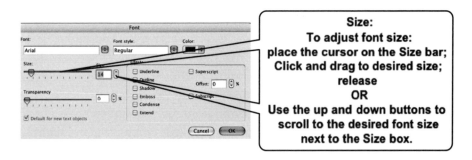

Class Portrait Page

If there is one group photo of the entire class, another page in the template, the Class Group Portrait page shown in Figure 13.9, may be employed.

Figure 13.9   The Class Group Portrait Page From the "Yearbook" Template

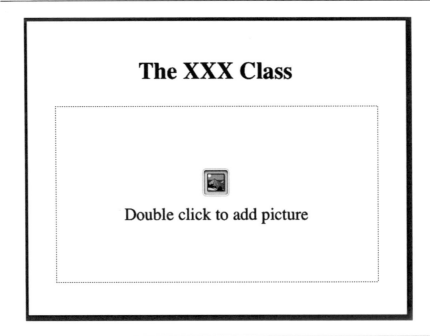

This page is designed for the user to delete the *X*'s and type in the class name. Then one large photo of the entire class can be imported by dragging a photo into the PowerPoint presentation. Save.

Monthly Birthday Pages

There are birthday pages for each month from September through June and additional pages for summer birthdays in July and August. Children and/or staff who celebrate birthdays during a particular month can have their photos, ages, and dates inserted on the appropriate page, as shown in Figure 13.10. Save.

If fewer than four children celebrated birthdays that month, the extra photo box(es) can be deleted by clicking on it and then deleting. To delete the text, highlight the text and delete. Photos and the text can be repositioned on the page by clicking on the photo or text box, waiting for the hand to appear, clicking such that the hand grasps the photo or box, dragging the box to the desired location on the page, and then releasing the mouse. Save.

Figure 13.10   A Birthday Page Before and After Entering Data

"Very Important Kid" Pages

There are pages in which to feature the Very Important Kid for each week of that month, as shown in Figure 13.11.

Figure 13.11   A "Very Important Kids" Page, Before and After Entering Data

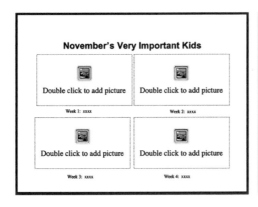

To use the Very Important Kids page, drag appropriate photos into appropriate boxes. Click on the text, delete the *X*'s, and type in the child's name. Save.

Monthly Activities Pages

Pages are available for each month. Photos of children engaged in activities or themes can be inserted on these pages, as shown in Figure 13.12. If the user wants to insert text to describe the photos, the Text Box function on the drawing toolbar should be used, as previously mentioned in this chapter and in Chapter 6. Save.

Figure 13.12   Monthly Activity Pages, Before and After Entering Data

Other Yearbook Pages

Other pages are available for inserting photos of field trips, guest speakers, or parent night activities. (See the examples in Figure 13.13.) If additional descriptive text is desired, the Text Box that is located in the drawing toolbar function should again be used.

Figure 13.13   Other Pages in the "Yearbook" Template

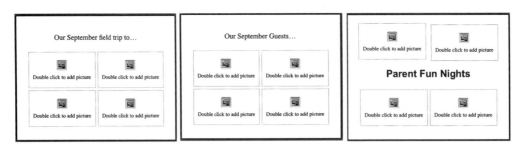

Always remember to save any work that has been completed.

Caution: Printing many pages of colored photos is expensive and time consuming. Therefore, it might be desirable to print many of the photos in black-and-white for ease in copying. Consult with a commercial printing business regarding how to duplicate and bind the yearbook. Another alternative is to sell the yearbook in electronic form on a CD.

T-Shirts

Another fundraising idea that employs digital photography is to produce T-shirts with a photographic image of the children in the class. One can purchase T-shirt transfers at a fabric store or office supply store and buy inexpensive, light-colored T-shirts at a discount department store or craft store. It is better to use light-colored fabrics, because the T-shirt photo transfers show up better on them. To produce a T-shirt transfer, use the PowerPoint program and select the large picture with print option, as shown in Figure 13.14.

Figure 13.14 The Large Picture With Print Page Option in PowerPoint

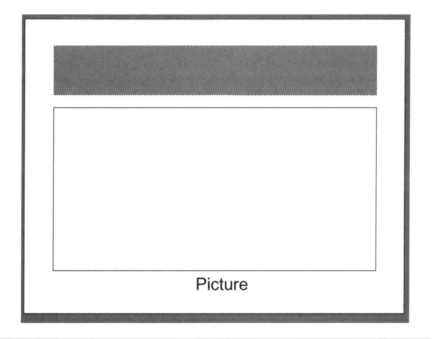

Picture

Drag in the desired photo. To flip the print, the WordArt program must be used. Select the WordArt option from the Drawing toolbar by moving the cursor to the toolbar and clicking (see Figure 13.15).

A pop-up array of different printing styles will appear. Choose one by clicking on it until it becomes highlighted and then click OK (see Figure 13.16 on page 203).

Another pop-up window will appear. Type in the title where it says "Your Text Here" (see Figure 13.17 on page 203).

The program will automatically center your text, but if you want to distinguish two lines, press the return bar at the end of a line.

Figure 13.15   Locating WordArt on the Drawing Toolbar

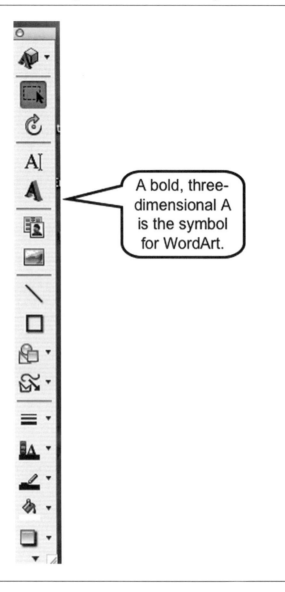

A bold, three-dimensional A is the symbol for WordArt.

Click on OK when you have the desired text. The text will pop into the PowerPoint and will need to be repositioned on the page by clicking on the text box and grabbing the box with the hand to move it into the appropriate space.

To reverse or mirror the text, grab a handle (small box) on a vertical side and drag it to the opposite side, as shown in Figure 13.18.

The text will be reversed (see Figure 13.19 on page 204). Move the cursor to the center of the print until the hand appears. Click the cursor

Figure 13.16   Choosing a WordArt Style

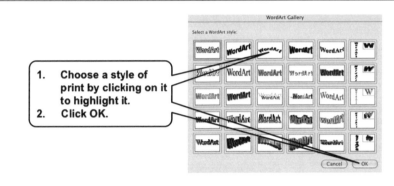

Figure 13.17   Before and After Entering Text Into the WordArt Program

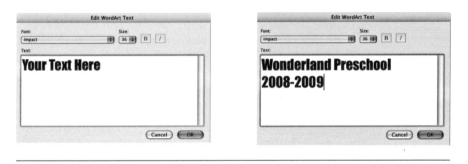

Figure 13.18   Reversing the Text for a T-shirt Transfer

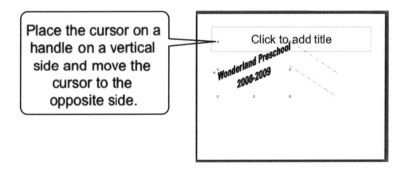

Figure 13.19   Reversed Print Image

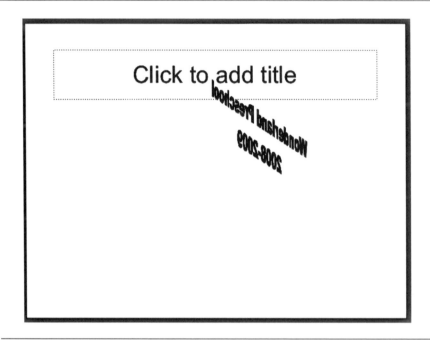

to grab and move the print so that it is centered or in another desired position on the page. Save.

Drag in a photo. If it does not matter which direction the photo is printed, the photo does not need to be reversed. However, if there is obvious lettering on a child's shirt, for instance, then the photo will need to be reversed. If the photo does need to be printed as pictured, click on the photo until boxes appear around the perimeter. Go to the Edit menu and scroll down to Duplicate (see Figure 13.20).

Figure 13.20   Duplicating a Photo

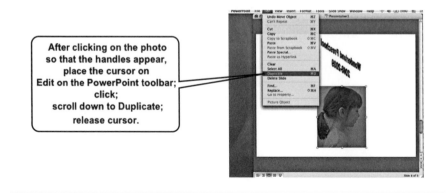

A second image will appear. Click on one of the photos until boxes appear around the perimeter. Now place the cursor on the photo until the hand appears. Move the photo such that one photo is above the other (see Figure 3.21).

Figure 13.21　Lining Up Photos to Ensure Same Size When Reversing Image

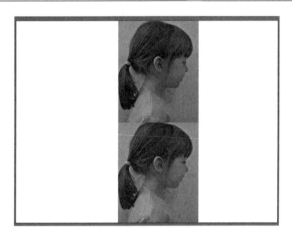

Click on one of the photos until boxes appear around the perimeter. Place the cursor on a center box (handle) on a vertical side; click and drag to the opposite side and beyond until the photo is flipped (see Figure 13.22).

Figure 13.22　Reversing an Image

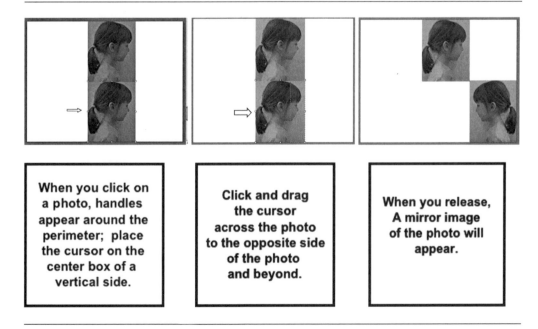

When you click on a photo, handles appear around the perimeter; place the cursor on the center box of a vertical side.

Click and drag the cursor across the photo to the opposite side of the photo and beyond.

When you release, A mirror image of the photo will appear.

Grab the reversed photo with the hand and move it directly over the original photo. Resize as necessary to avoid distortion (see Figure 13.23).

Figure 13.23   Lining Up Photos to Ensure Same Size to Avoid Distortion

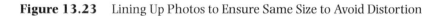

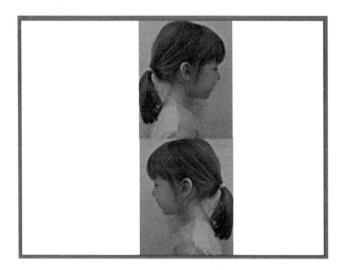

Click on original photo until boxes appear around the perimeter. Release. Press delete button. Photo will be deleted. Click on the remaining photo until the hand appears. Click and drag the photo into appropriate position on the page. Save. Print the image on a T-shirt transfer. Follow the directions on the T-shirt transfer package regarding prewashing the T-shirt, trimming the image, and ironing the image onto the T-shirt.

Quilt

Visit a fabric store and inquire about appropriate fabrics on which to print images; pellon can also be used. Select a variety of photos to depict the children and the activities for a school year. Print the photos on the fabric. Sew the pieces together to create a quilt that can be auctioned at a school's silent auction.

LOOKING BACK/LOOKING AHEAD

A digital camera can be a useful technological tool for teachers, children, parents, and staff. The information in this book should empower the reader to use photography in a variety of ways to boost parent communication, contribute to assessment, enhance children's learning, and assist with many other aspects of early childhood education. Photography is also an art that lends itself to further creativity.

Digital Images + Imagination = Possibilities

Imagine the possibilities that you, the reader, will discover as you use the tips and tools presented in this book to create with digital photography.

Glossary

ARCS motivational model: Developed by John M. Keller in 1993, an instructional model intended to guide educators in promoting and sustaining learner motivation in the classroom.

cables: Insulated strands of metal fibers or fiber optics used to transmit audio/video signals or small electrical currents, or both, to transfer data from one medium to another. Common cables used with digital photography include video-in/out, USB, and Firewire.

card reader: A device designed to read media cards (e.g., Compact Flash, Smart Media, SD Cards, and Memory Sticks) from digital media devices, such as digital cameras, and upload photos to a computer. Card readers typically connect to a computer via a USB port or are built into many of today's personal computers, laptops, and printers.

CD-R: Stands for "compact disc-recordable." A compact disc media format that allows one-time recording.

CD-RW: Stands for "compact disc-rewriteable." A compact disc media format that allows for repeated recording.

charge-coupled device (CCD): A device that converts an optical image, reflected from light, into electrical charges that result in a digital form of a document or object.

computer file: An electronic document for storing information. Computer files are available for software applications to use after the current software application has finished storing information.

cropping: A common editing function that is used to cut off unwanted parts of a digital photograph.

developmental domains: Areas of child development. Typical domains include cognitive development, emotional development, language development, motor development, and social development.

digital camera: A camera that captures and stores pictures digitally rather than on photographic film. Digital photos are stored on storage media devices and then transferred to a computer for display or manipulation.

dock*:* A panel on Macintosh's OS X·operating system that provides quick access to some applications. The dock indicates which Macintosh applications are running and holds windows in their minimized state.

GIF: An acronym for *Graphical Interchange Format.* A widely used image format used on the World Wide Web that is suitable for digital graphics with sharp edges and relatively few gradations of color (e.g., line art, cartoons, and text). Most e-mail environments are capable of displaying gif image formats.

handles: The small boxes around the perimeter of a text box or photo box within the PowerPoint program that are used for resizing.

hyperlink: An element of an electronic document that links, or connects, to another place within the same document or to a different document. Hyperlinks are a key component of Web pages.

HyperStudio: A multimedia authoring program that allows users to combine text, graphics, animation, video, and audio to communicate ideas to others.

image editing software: Software applications that allow a user to alter, enhance, or add special effects to digital images and photos.

image management software: Software applications that allow a user easily to identify, organize, and distribute digital images and photos.

inkjet printers: A type of nonimpact printer that sprays small drops of black and/or color ink onto a physical medium, such as paper, to produce graphics and text.

iPhoto: An Apple Inc. software application for Mac OS X operating systems designed to import, organize, edit, print, and share digital photos.

JPEG: An acronym for *Joint Photographic Expert Group.* A common file format for compressed digital images and photos to save storage space. Most e-mail environments are capable of displaying jpeg image formats.

language experience chart: A teacher's written transcription of the children's exact words as they dictate about an experience or field trip, typically written on chart paper.

laser printer: A high-speed, nonimpact printer that utilizes a laser beam to produce text and graphics on a medium, such as paper.

LCD: An acronym for *liquid crystal display*. A type of display that uses two sheets of polarizing material with a liquid crystal solution between them. An electric current passes through this liquid solution, causing crystals to align so that light can or can't pass through them, resulting in moving images. Display screen on the digital camera.

magnet sheet: An office paper product that has a magnetic backing.

mechanical resolution: A type of resolution set by a motor inside a scanner that controls the charge-coupled device (CCD) that defines a scanned document's dots-per-inch (dpi) that run vertically in electronic format.

megapixel: One million pixels.

nonimpact printers: A category of printers that place marks on a physical medium, such as paper, without striking the medium.

pellon: Translucent fabric that may be used as a medium on which to print photos; may be used to create pieces for a flannelboard story.

pattern book: A book for emergent readers in which the same basic sentence is repeated from page to page; the beginning string of words remains the same, but the final word is changed.

photo paper: A type of paper with a special coating for printing photographs on an inkjet printer.

photo printer: A type of nonimpact printer designed to produce professional-quality color photo prints.

picture book: A book for young children that allocates more space to pictures than to text; the pictures provide a context for interpreting the words in the storyline.

pixel: A single dot, black or in color, in a picture captured by a digital camera; also known as a "picture element."

presentation graphics software: Software applications tools that allow users to create presentations to communicate ideas, messages, and other information to a specific target audience.

printer: An output device that produces text and graphics on a physical medium, such as paper or transparency sheets.

PowerPoint: A multimedia presentation graphics application made by Microsoft for creating presentations, speeches, and slides. PowerPoint is used to create linear and nonlinear professional presentations and offers word processing, drawing, graphing, and management tools.

resizing: A common editing function that is used to increase or decrease the size of the visual appearance of a digital photograph.

resolution: The spacing of pixels in a digital photograph, which is measured in pixels per inch (ppi) or commonly referred to as dots per inch (dpi).

scanner: An input device that can be used to create electronic versions of print-based or physical objects, including instructional materials such as drawings, photographs, and magazine clippings.

social story: A brief, personalized story that identifies a desirable behavior or skill, often told with pictures, that demonstrates what to do and affirms that the child can do the behavior or skill.

storage device: Technological apparatus for storing and retrieving data, such as text or images, to and from a storage medium. Some examples of storage devices include Zip drives, jump drives, CD/DVD drives, USB flash drives, and floppy disk drives.

storage media: Material on which data is kept, such as CDs, DVDs, flash memory cards, floppy disks, Zip disks, and hard disks.

template: A document or file having a preset format, which is used as a starting point for a particular application so that the format does not have to be recreated each time it is used.

thumbnails: Small digital pictorials representing the same larger version of a graphic or image. Thumbnails provide quick access to larger graphics or images for viewing or manipulation.

TIFF: An acronym for *Tag Image File Format.* A common file format for uncompressed digital images and photos that maintains high-quality results.

USB port: An acronym for *universal serial bus.* A small, rectangular wire external port used to carry low-speed data and provide power to some computer hardware peripherals.

video out: A video interface offered on most audiovisual equipment (e.g., VHS, DVD, and digital cameras) used to send and receive analog video signals.

Web page: A document on the World Wide Web, or the Web, consisting of an HTML file and any related files for scripts and graphics and often hyperlinked to other documents on the Web. The content of Web pages is normally accessed by using a Web browser.

whole child: The sum of the parts related to cognitive development, emotional development, fine motor development, language and literacy development, large motor development, self-help skills development, and social development.

Windows Media Video (WMV): A highly compressed video format developed by Microsoft designed to work with Windows Media Player. WMV video is a common format found on the World Wide Web.

wordless picture book: A book that tells a story through illustrations or photos rather than through words.

List of Forms on the CD

Checklist of Permissions

Photo Release Form

Record Keeping: Photos of Children's Bodies

Record Keeping: Photos of Children's Development

Record Keeping: Photos of Children's Faces

Record Keeping: Special Events Photos

List of Templates on the CD

ABCs of Names Template

Address and Phone Template

Celebrating Template

Children's Recipes Template

Counting Fruits Template

County Fair Template

Daily Schedule Template

Dancing Popcorn Process Chart Template

Day at School Template

Eating Fruits Template

Eating Vegetables Template

Family Vacation Template

Favorite Activities Template

Feelings Template

Friend of Mine Template

Hello Template

I Go to School Template

Newsletter Template

Newsnote Template

Our School Year

Paperclips Tall Template

Passport Template

Playground Template

Portfolio Template

Star Template

Star of the Week Template

Ten Little Friends Template

Trip to Farm Template

Trip to Zoo Template

Valentine Template

Very Important Kid Certificate Template

We Can Read Template

We Have Animals Template

We Like Colors Template

We Like Shapes Template

Yearbook Template

URLs Cited by Chapter

Chapter 1

http://www.mprove.de/diplom/text/3.2.2_threestages.html

http://www.naeyc.org/about/positions/PSTECH98.asp

http://www.naeyc.org/faculty/pdf/2001.pdf

http://www.netc.org/earlyconnections/byrequest.html

Chapter 2

http://www.dcresource.com

http://www.shortcourses.com/index.htm

http://www.digitalcamerainfo.com

http://www.dpreview.com/learn/?/Glossary/Camera_System/storage_card_01.htm

http://www.epinions.com/buyers_guide/Digital_Cameras_buyers_guide_p1.html

http://review.zdnet.com/4566-3155_16-0.html http://www.microsoft.com/windowsxp/using/digitalphotography/getstarted/newPC.mspx

http://photo.net/equipment/digital/computers/

http://www.buyerzone.com/computers/scanners/buyers_guide1.html

http://www.pcworld.com/article/id,102514-page,2-c,scanners/article.html

http://graphicssoft.about.com/od/imagemanagement/Image_Management_Image_Viewers_Organizers_Databases.htm

http://www.imaging-resource.com/SOFT.HTM

http://www.iloveschools.com

http://www.theteacherswishlist.com

Chapter 3

http://www.photoshare.org/phototips/developethics.php

http://www.indiana.edu/~edrsch/checklist.html

http://ww.wsd1.org/board/policies_pdf/policy_KBAA.pdf

Chapter 4

http://www.polaroid.com

Chapter 5

http://home.earthlink.net/~cnew/research.htm

http://www.princetonol.com/groups/iad/links/clipart.html

http://www.clipart.com

http://classroomclipart.com/CRCLcopyright.htm

Chapter 7

http://www.thegraycenter.org/store/

http://rsaffran.tripod.com/social.html

Chapter 8

http://www.headstartinfo.org/leaders_guideeng/domain6.htm

Chapter 9

http://www.naeyc.org/about/positions/psread2.asp

http://www.naeyc.org/about/positions/psread1.asp

http://groups.yahoo.com/group/boardmaker/

http://www.mayer-johnson.com

http://www97.intel.com/en/ProjectDesign/UnitPlanIndex/FlatStanley/

http://www.oct.ca/publications/professionally_speaking/september_1998/brain.htm

Chapter 10

http://standards.nctm.org/document/chapter4/index.htm

http://crafts.kaboose.com/handpoem.html

http://www.dltk-holidays.com/dad/mhandprintalt.html

http://www.dltk-holidays.com/mom/mhandprintpoem.htm

Chapter 11

http://mason.gmu.edu/~montecin/powerpoint.html

http://smilebox.com

Chapter 12

http://www.highscope.org

http://www.teachingstrategies.com/bookshop/

http://www.portageproject.org/brochure/Orderfrm.htm

http://thechp.syr.edu/checklist_download.html

http://www.kcentric.com/Parent/Developmental/Checklists/
DevelopmentalChecklists.htm

http://www.education-world.com/standards/state/index.shtml

Chapter 13

http://cameras.about.com/od/digitalcameragifts/tp/camerasforkids
.htm

http://holidays.about.com/od/giftsforkids/tp/camerasforkids.htm

http://www.youthlearn.org/learning/activities/multimedia/photo1.asp

http://www.wacona.com/digicam/digicam.html

References

Allen, K. Eileen, & Marotz, Lynn R. (2007). *Developmental profiles pre-birth through twelve* (5th ed.). Clifton Park, NY: Thomson Delmar Learning.

Andreae, Giles (with Wojtowycz, David, Illustrator). (2001). *Rumble in the jungle.* New York: Simon and Schuster Books for Young Children.

Beaty, Janice J. (1992) *Preschool Appropriate Practices.* Fort Worth, TX: Harcourt Brace Jovanovich College Publishers.

Bidner, Jenni. (2004). *The kid's guide to digital photography: How to shoot, save, play with & print your digital photos.* Asheville, NC: Lark Books.

Brown, Jeff. (2003). *Flat Stanley.* New York: Harper Collins.

Browne, Ron. (2005/2006, Winter). It's a snap! Selecting the right digital camera. *Childhood Education, 82*(2), 86–88.

Caine, Renate, & Caine, Geoffrey. (1994) *Making connections.* New York: Addison Wesley.

Carle, Eric. (1969). *The very hungry caterpillar.* New York: Scholastic Books.

DeMarie, Darlene. (2001, Spring). A trip to the zoo: Children's words and photographs. *Early Childhood Research and Practice, 3*(1). Available April 4, 2008, at http://ecrp.uiuc.edu/v3n1/demarie.html

DeMarie, Darlene, & Ethridge, Elizabeth A. (2006, January). Children's images of preschool: The power of photography. *Young Children, 61*(1), 101–104.

Digital photography for kids (kids essentials). (2006). Northamptonshire, United Kingdom: Igloo Books.

Dodge, Diane Trister, Colker, Laura J., & Heroman, Cate. (2002). *The creative curriculum for preschool* (4th ed.). Washington, DC: Teaching Strategies.

Donohue, Chip. (2003, November/December). Technology in early childhood education. *Child Care Information Exchange, 17*–22.

Drake, Pamela. (n.d.). *Woodkins.* Berkeley, CA: Author. Retrieved April 4, 2008, from http://www.woodkins.com

Duncan, Deborah. (n.d.). *Using a digital camera in the classroom.* Retrieved April 4, 2008, from http://www.wam.umd.edu/~toh/image/DigitalCameraUses.htm

Entz, Susan, & Galarza, Sheri Lyn. (2000). *Picture this: Digital and instant photography activities for early childhood learning.* Thousand Oaks, CA: Corwin Press.

Erikson, Erik. (1963). *Childhood and society* (2nd ed.). New York: Norton.

Ewald, Wendy, & Lightfoot, Alexandra. (2003). *I wanna take me a picture: Teaching photography and writing to children.* Boston: Beacon.

Finkelstein, Ellen. (2007). *How to do everything with Microsoft Office PowerPoint 2007.* New York: McGraw-Hill.

Friedman, Debra. (2003). *Picture this: Fun photography and crafts (kids can do it).* Tonawanda, NY: Kids Can Press.

Gagné, R. (1985). *The conditions of learning* (4th ed.). New York: Holt, Rinehart and Wilson.

Gagné, R., Briggs, L., & Wager, W. (1992). *Pinciples of instructional design* (4th ed.). Fort Worth, TX: HBJ College Publishers.

Gardner, Howard. (1983). *Frames of mind: Theory of multiple intelligences.* New York: Basic Books.

Gardner, Howard, & Hatch, Thomas. (1989). Multiple intelligences go to school. *Educational Researcher, 18*(8), 4–10.

Geyer, Beth, & Geyer, Frank. (2005). *Teaching early concepts with photos of kids.* New York: Scholastic.

Goleman, Daniel. (1995). *Emotional intelligence.* New York: Bantam Books.

Good, Linda. (2005/2006, Winter). Snap it up! Using digital photography in early childhood. *Childhood Education, 82*(2), 79–85.

Gordon, Anne Miles, & Browne, Kathryn Williams. (2004). *Beginnings & beyond: Foundations in early childhood education* (6th ed.). Clifton Park, NY: Delmar Learning.

Healy, Jane M. (1990). *Endangered minds: Why children don't think and what we can do about it.* New York: Touchstone.

Hoisington, Cynthia. (2002, September). Using photographs to support children's science inquiry. *Young Children,* 26–32.

International Society for Technology in Education. (2000). *National educational technology standards for students: Connecting curriculum and technology.* Eugene, OR: Author.

Jalongo, Mary Renck, & Isenberg, Joan P. (2004). *Exploring your role: A practitioner's introduction to early childhood education* (2nd ed.). Upper Saddle River, NJ: Pearson/Merrill Prentice Hall.

Keller, J. M. (1983). Motivational design of instruction. In C. M. Reigeluth (Ed.), *Instructional design theories and models: An overview of their current status.* Hillsdale, NJ: Lawrence Erlbaum Associates.

Keller, J. M. (1987). Development and use of the ARCS model of motivation in teacher training. In K. Shaw & A. J. Trott (Eds.), *Aspects of educational technology: Vol. 17. Staff development and career updating.* London: Kogan Page.

Lawrence, Michael. (2005). *Tips & tricks for using digital photography.* Westminster, CA: Teacher Created Resources.

Lehman, Barbara. (2004). *The red book.* New York: Scholastic.

LeSieg, Theo. (1989) *Ten apples up on top!* New York: Random House Beginner Books. (Original work published 1961)

Lever-Duffy, J., & McDonald, J. B. (2008). *Teaching and learning with technology* (3rd ed.). Boston: Allyn & Bacon

Lowe, Doug. (2007). *Microsoft Office PowerPoint 2007 for dummies.* Hoboken, NJ: Wiley Publishing.

Martin, Jr., Bill, & Carle, Eric. (1995). *Brown bear, brown bear, what do you see?* New York: Henry Holt.

Maslow, Abraham. (1968). *Toward a psychology of being* (2nd ed.). Princeton, NJ: Van Nostrand.

Matthews, Carole. (2004). *Microsoft Office Powerpoint 2003: Quick steps.* New York: McGraw-Hill/Osborne.

McAfee, Oralie, & Leong, Deborah J. (2007) *Assessing and guiding young children's development and learning* (4th ed.). Boston: Pearson Education.

Mindes, Gayle. (2007). *Assessing young children* (3rd ed.). Upper Saddle River, New Jersey: Pearson/Merrill Prentice Hall.

Montessori, Maria. (1964). *The Montessori method.* New York: Schocken Books.

Muir, Nancy. (2006). *Teach yourself visually: The fast and easy way to learn Microsoft PowerPoint 2003.* Hoboken, NJ: Wiley Publishing.

Murphy, Karen L., DePasquale, Roseanne, & McNamara, Erin. (2003, November). Meaningful connections: Using technology in primary classrooms. *Young Children, 58*(6), 12–18.

National Association for the Education of Young Children (NAEYC). (2008) *Draft NAEYC Position Statement: Developmentally Appropriate Practice in Early Childhood Programs Serving Children From Birth to Age 8.* Washington, DC: Author.

Negrino, Tom. (2007). *Creating a presentation in Microsoft Office PowerPoint 2007 for Windows.* Berkeley, CA: Peachpit Press.

Neumann-Hinds, Carla. (2007). *Picture science: Using digital photography to teach young children.* St. Paul, MN: Redleaf Press.

Numeroff, Laura. (1998). *If you give a mouse a cookie.* New York: Scholastic.

Online Training Solutions, Inc. (2004). *Step by Step Microsoft PowerPoint 2003* (with CD). Redmond, WA: Microsoft Press.

Park, John. (2002). *Digital camera characteristics.* Retrieved April 4, 2008, from http://www.ncsu.edu/sciencejunction/route/usetech/digitalcamera/index.html

Pastor, Ella, & Kerns, Emily. (1997, November). A digital snapshot of an early childhood classroom. *Educational Leadership,* 42–45.

Perspection, Inc., & Pinard, K. (1999). *Step by Step Microsoft PowerPoint 2000* (with CD). Redmond, WA: Microsoft Press.

Piaget, Jean. (1952). *The origins of intelligence in children.* New York: Norton.

Puckett, Margaret B., & Black, Janet K. (2005). *The young child: Development from prebirth through age eight* (4th ed.). Upper Saddle River, NJ: Pearson/Merrill Prentice Hall.

Raines, Shirley C., & Canady, Robert J. (1989). *Story S_T_R_E_T_C_H_E_R_S: Activities to expand children's favorite books.* Mt. Rainier, MD: Gryphon House.

Shelly, G. B., Cashman, T. J., Gunter, G. A., & Gunter, R. E. (2006). *Teachers discovering computers: Integrating technology and digital media in the classroom* (4th ed.). Boston: Thomson Course Technology.

Singer, Dorothy G., & Revenson, T. A. (1996). *A Piaget primer: How a child thinks.* New York: Plume.

Slobodkina, Esphyr. (1989) *Caps for sale.* New York: Scholastic. (Original work published 1940)

Smaldino, S. E., Lowther, D. L., & Russell, J. D. (2008). *Instructional technology and media for learning* (9th ed.). Upper Saddle River, NJ: Merrill Prentice Hall.

Spier, Peter (Illustrator). (1977). *Noah's ark.* New York: Scholastic.

Sponseller, D. B., & Chisolm, M., Johnson, M., Plum, N., & Stenger, B. (1979, April). *Photographic feedback effects on preschool exceptional children's self-concept and self-confidence.* Paper presented at the 57th Annual International Convention, The Council for Exceptional Children, Dallas, TX.

Starr, Linda. (2002, October 16). *Quick! Get the (digital) camera!* Retrieved April 4, 2008, from http://www.education-world.com/a_tech/tech/tech148.shtml

Starr, Linda. (2004, November 10). *Smile! Digital cameras can make your day.* Retrieved April 4, 2008, from http://www.education-world.com/a_tech/tech/tech147.shtml

Turkle, Brinton. (1976). *Deep in the forest.* New York: Dutton Books.

Twinn, M. (with Adams, P., Illustrator). (1992). *Ten beads tall.* Singapore: National Curriculum.

Vygotsky, L.S. (1978) *Mind in society. The development of higher psychological processes.* Cambridge, MA: Harvard University.

Walker, Tim, & Donohue, C. (2006a, May/June). Decoding technology: Choosing a digital camera. *Exchange* (169), 22–23.

Walker, Tim, & Donohue, C. (2006b, July/August). Decoding technology: Digital cameras in the early childhood program. *Exchange* (170), 66–67.

Warren, Jean. *Totline piggyback songs.* Retrieved April 4, 2008, from www.bestwebbuys.com/Piggyback_Songs-ISBN_9780911019018.html?isrcb-search

Wempen, Faithe. (2007). *Microsoft PowerPoint 2007 bible.* Indianapolis, IN: Wiley.

Wolfe, Patricia. (2001). *Brain matters: Translating research into classroom practice.* Alexandria, VA: Association for Supervision and Curriculum Development.

Wood, A. (with Wood, D., Illustrator). (1984). *The napping house.* New York: Scholastic.

Index

CORWIN PRESS

The Corwin Press logo—a raven striding across an open book—represents the union of courage and learning. Corwin Press is committed to improving education for all learners by publishing books and other professional development resources for those serving the field of PreK–12 education. By providing practical, hands-on materials, Corwin Press continues to carry out the promise of its motto: **"Helping Educators Do Their Work Better."**